D0517240

MORE SPACE

Nine Antidotes To Complacency In Business

Edited by Todd Sattersten

CONTRIBUTING AUTHORS:

Jory Des Jardins

Lisa Haneberg

Rob May

Johnnie Moore

Marc Orchant

Robert Paterson

Evelyn Rodriguez

Curt Rosengren

Jeremy Wright

FIRST EDITION

Astronaut
PROJECTS

USA

Published by:

Astronaut Projects, LLC
info@astroprojects.com
http://www.astroprojects.com

Cover photograph by: Leah-Anne Thompson

ISBN 0-9770048-3-X
Library of Congress Control Number 2005928930

First Edition 2005 Softcover
Printed in the USA

CONTENTS

Stuff That Makes You Think

----

by Seth Godin

For a culture that spends so much time writing and talking and spouting and yelling, we don't say very much.

Nine times out of ten, it's stuff you've heard before. Stuff you already agree with, or have decided to disagree with, or want to ignore.

Too much noise, not enough signal.

Maybe you can find the good stuff in magazines. Nope, that won't work. All you'll find is another picture of Warren or Jack or Bill. Or another puff piece about something you already know about.

What about blogs? Aren't blogs the next frontier in big thinking?

Maybe, at least for a while. But with 20,000,000 blogs out there, you've got to wade through a lot of blogrolls and flame wars and parroting before you find something you'd like to read.

Which brings me to this book. I'd call it "Less Noise" not "More Space." Every single article, even the ones you don't like, is worth thinking about. Every single author has something new and interesting to say.

For me, that's more than enough. New and interesting are in short supply. Have fun.

INTRODUCTION
I Had This Idea . . .

- -

by Todd Sattersten

I am one of those people who constantly come up with ideas. Of course, most of mine feel like crummy ideas after I get a chance to ponder them. Even more I will never act on.

But *More Space* got past all the filters.

I wanted to see what would happen if you gave business bloggers more space to develop the ideas they write about every day. The trouble with weblogs is that they are best for short-form writing. Each entry is normally a couple of hundred words containing a single thought—and that thought is normally a response to something someone else has written.

So I asked some of my favorite business bloggers to write 5,000 to 10,000 words on a business topic they were interested in, and the results are amazing:

PASSION.

AUTHENTICITY.

PRODUCTIVITY.

CHANGE.

COMMUNITY.

SIMPLICITY.

INNOVATION.

PERSPECTIVE.

I think the ideas contained in this book match a set of sensibilities that have growing importance in business today. None of these ideas are new, but the emphasis that needs to be placed on them is. The marketplace is full of products and messages, most of which no one wants to hear about.

Imagine This Story, Though—

You start by building a fire and sending up some smoke signals. You find people who are passionate about the stuff you do. You hire some of them and start a conversation with the rest about their hopes and dreams and desires and frustrations. You talk to them in a plainspoken way about what you are capable of and what you as a company are trying to become. More people start checking you out, wanting to know more about your company and about you and your employees. As the group around the campfire grows, you start to look inward and see you're not set up for this type of gig. You need to reconstruct the construct. You need to be constantly putting stuff out there to see if it flies or fades. You have to get more done in less time. You need to understand you are never done.

But where do you start?

More Space contains stories of the past, present, and future. If you are tired, complacent, or just seeking something different, read on. Find yourself and your business within these essays. Then keep reading until you find an idea you can implement today— an idea that will re-ignite your passion for business.

★   ★   ★   ★

More Space also draws on some important ideas beyond the basic blog expansion.

The project had to be a book. Books have a historical quality, and these ideas needed to be captured and recorded. The length of the pieces individually and certainly when combined is beyond the usual tolerance for online reading. And above all, ideas on paper still hold a level of credibility that ones on computer screens don't.

This book had to be self-published. Publishers look for writers with platforms. These bloggers are just people with ideas. With mainstream publishing, we would have given up things like the color photographs and the sounds of our voices. For writers who self-publish their work every day, how could the book not be self-published?

The basic concepts had to be free. You probably found us through the free material on the *More Space* web site (www.astroprojects.com/morespace). This is meant to be another example of how you can give content away— and, as Seth says, people will buy the souvenirs. The Creative Commons copyright license takes it another step further, allowing even more sharing and more freedom.

Citizen media.

Generation C.

Whatever you call it.

At the base of all this is people creating content and sharing it with the world.

Why Business Matters

----

by Rob May

I only need to drink five more beers. I've downed twenty-five so far, not all tonight, but over the last two months. Once I drink all thirty that they offer, I get a free T-shirt. That is the deal. Five beers shouldn't be difficult. I come here once a week. Most of us come every week. You have to if you are a real fan.

I always start off the night with the beer I think I will like the least. I can get a good one later. I grab it as soon as I walk in the door and then head downstairs. We meet downstairs so that we don't bother any of the restaurant's other patrons. I chat with my friends as they arrive. We exchange stories about what happened this week and what we think will happen tonight. Sometimes a few fair-weather fans show up here too, and I usually introduce myself to them.

The excitement builds as the meeting gets started because . . . well, we are all just so into this. But the meeting I attend every Tuesday night in downtown Louisville usually has nothing to do with sports, or music, or television. We are a fan club, but an unusual one. The meeting is called Bizjunkies, and it is for people like me—people who like to get together over dinner and a few beers and talk business.

Very few people like business this much, which is strange, because it is a popular field. But business books do not sell as well as most other types of books. Business periodicals do not have the subscription rates one would expect, given how many people are involved in business. And I don't know about you, but when I'm out and about I rarely hear conversations about business. It's almost as if people think business doesn't matter. Nothing could be further from the truth.

Sports fans are easy to find—the bars are filled with them any time there is a game. Business fans, judging from the size of our weekly meeting, number much fewer. Yet we talk with just as much passion—because to us, business is a sport, and so much more. It's got winners and losers, action and strategy, but unlike sports, it has the power to do good or do harm. At its best, it is metaphor for living well. That is why I feel so strongly that business matters.

FALLING IN LOVE

We are shaped and fashioned by what we love.
—Goethe

I remember as a kid that my mother would be in the middle of a conversation and, if she didn't want us kids to know something she would write it down in cursive. Sometimes, especially if it had to do with a gift she had bought, I would stare and try to make sense of it, but I never could. Then in the third grade I learned how to read and write cursive and this whole new world opened up to me. Things that were hidden had become visible. All these random markings around me suddenly had meaning. They suddenly made sense. It was the first eye-opening experience I remember. It wouldn't be my last.

I love business. It excites me so much that it's odd to think that I ended up on this path almost by accident. When I enrolled in the electrical engineering program at the University of Kentucky, I had no intention of pursuing a business degree because, well, to be honest, I wasn't really sure what I would do with it. I didn't know many businesspeople and the few I did know were salesmen. I equated a business degree with sales, and that did not sound like an appealing career path.

The university had just started offering a joint degree program that allowed students to get an undergraduate degree in engineering along with an MBA. I don't really remember why I applied. I think it was just another way to keep my options open for the future. The country was just coming out of a recession and jobs were scarce. I thought having degrees in two different fields might give me more job opportunities when I graduated. They only took a handful of students each year and whether I made it on merit or because it was new and short of applicants I will never know.

I took the GMAT and scored high enough that I could go ahead and begin my graduate-level business courses without finishing my undergraduate degree. I enjoyed mixing my program with both business and engineering classes. Each gave me a break from the other and kept me from getting bogged down and bored with too much of the same thing. Early on, I had to take a graduate-level economics course. The professor passed out some student discount forms for the Wall Street Journal and it seemed like a good deal, so I signed up. I thought that if the world's most successful people read this thing daily, maybe I should too. I began reading it reluctantly, mostly for class rather than anything else. I did not have the background to follow much of what was talked about in the various articles, but over time it began to make more and more sense to me. Then a funny thing happened. I began to see business around me—everywhere. It was always there, I'd just never noticed it before. It was like learning cursive all over again.

Once I developed such a strong interest in business, I could not go to the grocery without taking note of product displays, what was on sale, and how the store was laid out. As I shopped, I wondered how and why these decisions were made. I often asked managers questions like "I see those Cheerios are on the middle row now. Have you been selling more of them since you moved them up?" They probably thought I was crazy.

I began to ask my friends about what they did at work. I wanted specifics. We were in college so many of them were just bartenders or retail clerks or delivery drivers, but I pried into the operations of their workplaces. I became fascinated with how and why companies did things, and how consumers were affected by their decisions (including me, which was more important). Some people really didn't care to talk about it and found it totally uninteresting to discuss such things. It made me wonder why everyone else didn't like business so much.

WHY PEOPLE DON'T LIKE BUSINESS

I find it rather easy to portray a businessman. Being bland, rather cruel and incompetent comes naturally to me.
—John Cleese

A strange dichotomy surrounds the subject of business. It's a popular major at most colleges and universities, and it's a popular profession. But at the same time, it's rare to hear the average person mention anything positive about business. Why is that?

I see two reasons. The philosophical reason is that profits are not a noble goal. The personal reason is that work sucks.

We believe businesses exist for profit, and we have been taught that profit is bad. But neither statement is true. Businesses exist to serve the needs of a customer. Profit is a requirement to stay in business and continue serving those needs. Peter Drucker puts it eloquently (quoted in *The Essential Drucker*):

> Profit is not the explanation, cause or rationale of business behavior and business decisions, but rather the test of their validity. If archangels instead of businessmen sat in director's chairs, they would still have to be concerned with profitability, despite their total lack of personal interest in profit.

I won't defend the handful of companies that manipulate profits with accounting tricks, and I won't defend the few companies that manipulate markets and unique situations to take advantage of people. Once you throw out the frauds, I think that overall, profit is a measure of the usefulness of a company to society. Again Peter Drucker sums it up well in *The Post Capitalist Society*:

> A business that does not show a profit at least equal to its cost of capital is irresponsible; it wastes society's resources. Economic profit performance is the base without which business cannot discharge any other responsibilities, cannot be a good employer, a good citizen, a good neighbor.

The more demand there is for a product or service, the higher the price. The more efficient the company can be in producing the product or service, the cheaper the cost. Profit is the difference between price and cost. So strong profits indicate that as a company, you are producing something consumers want (high demand) and you are doing it efficiently (low cost). I think that is admirable.

The second reason that people don't like business is that work sucks. Most people I've known and worked with only work a fraction of their day. They spend time daydreaming, chatting with colleagues, surfing the Web, anything to avoid work. They avoid work because they find it unstimulating and devoid of meaning. I know I've felt that way at many of the jobs that I've had.

In college I worked for Radio Shack. One big component of their sales training involved stepping customers up to the next price level. If they were considering a $75 VCR, I was supposed to point them to the $85 VCR and explain all the extra features and benefits it would provide. I did this a few times, and I didn't think it worked very well, so I stopped. I focused on selling customers what they wanted. My manager was not too pleased and repeatedly pointed out to me the extra money I could make by stepping people up to the next level. But what I found was that when I tried upselling customers to the next price point, they often got upset and left to "think it over." Other times they might buy it only to regret later that they spent more money than they intended to. While I really enjoyed selling when it consisted of trying to meet customer needs, I hated it when the goal was to maximize the price of a single transaction. Yet that is what I was continually chided about. My manager made a job that I liked into a headache. For me, work sucked.

Basically, many people think that the motives of businesses are bad, and the experience of working for a business is bad too. The only thing positive some of them would say is that business gives them a paycheck.

As someone who is passionate about business for its own sake, I simply don't believe it has to be like this. Business can be exciting, rewarding, and fulfilling. It can inspire passion, drive progress in both technology and society, and make the world a better place. The first step toward a better vision of business is to realize that the effects of business are everywhere.

The Power Of Business

Nearly all men can stand adversity, but if you want to test a man's character, give him power.
—Abraham Lincoln

Business influences much of what we do. Through the allocation of both human and financial capital, businesses generate tremendous effects on the economy and society. But might does not make right, and businesses often make poor choices with negative consequences. Remember Enron?

Business And Society

Consumers drive trends with what they buy. Businesses drive trends with what they offer. Business affects society by defining the options from which consumers can choose. You can't buy mustard-flavored cola. Nobody makes it. While your options for a carbonated beverage may be many, you don't have an unlimited choice. At some level, a group of executives must decide what flavor combinations are most likely to succeed and therefore are worth pursuing. If you are in the minority that likes mustard-flavored beverages, you lose out if the company thinks more people would prefer their soft drinks flavored with lemon. Companies can only offer a limited assortment of stuff, no matter what the category, and the assortment that exists defines and shapes the future of society.

A friend of mine used to be fascinated by Bioré nose strips. These strips are placed on your wet nose and left for several minutes. When they are removed, the dirt in your pores goes with them. He always pointed out that consumers weren't sitting around clamoring for pore cleaning nose strips. Soaps and cleansers to clean pores on the entire face were already abundant. Yet when Bioré released these strips, they were a huge hit. Consumers did not demand them, but once the option was available, consumers embraced it. Skin-cleansing habits were changed forever.

Businesses also create standards. Often these standards continue to exist after the need for them is gone, but no one ever questions them. We get used to it and accept it. The QWERTY keyboard is a great example of this.

In the early days of manual typewriters, if the typist was too fast, the typewriter would jam—the type bars would get tangled up and the typist would have to stop and fix the problem. The solution that typewriter manufacturers devised was the QWERTY keyboard, which is the layout most of us still use. In this layout, commonly used letters are spread out to make typing as slow as possible, so that typewriter jams are minimized. It was a good idea at the time, but we don't need it today. We only stick with it because we are used to the standard.

Businesses set trends by what they offer. The most prominent examples are the technological innovations they create. Microsoft introduced a standard operating system that made it simple for anyone to use a computer. I remember the days before Windows. My neighbor had a Commodore that we used to play video games. To play a game, we had to spend an hour typing in strange codes out of a book. If we made a single mistake it wouldn't run and we had to type them all over again. The machine was hard to use, which is why very few people owned computers.

Windows changed all that. Computer users no longer had to navigate a file system using text commands at a C: prompt. Now they could do it visually, just like they navigate a real filing cabinet. They no longer had to remember arcane commands to launch programs—they just clicked on an icon. It made much more sense, and led to a dramatic increase in the acceptance of computers as tools that could increase productivity.

Sony introduced the Walkman and changed the way we listened to music. Apple introduced the iPod and changed the way we listened to music again. Amazon changed the way we buy books. Google changed the way we find information. Technology changes society, and business is a primary driver of new technologies.

Business And Individuals

Management is nothing more than motivating other people.
—Lee Iacocca

Work affects us. That is why business matters. Negative work experiences lead to negative attitudes.

Most of us spend more than a third of our waking hours at work each week. That work environment affects us. Managers in particular can either draw the best out of people or make their lives miserable. Far too often, it is the latter. The negative views of business I held as a teenager were largely shaped by a bad experience with one of my first managers.

I used to work in a restaurant for a guy named Mike. Mike always seemed to have a chip on his shoulder. He also seemed too smart to just be running a fast food restaurant. I think he felt the same way, and took his frustrations with his own life out on the employees he managed. Mike was never concerned with what people wanted, only with what he thought was best for them in his own mind.

New employees were required to have training in five key areas over a period of six months, and I was the trainer. I had done most of the training for quite some time. But Mike thought I was too flexible. I've always believed that people learn in many different ways and my goal with training was to ensure certain outcomes. How each person was trained did not matter to me and no two training sessions were alike because no two employees were alike. Mike wouldn't have it. The training had to be standardized.

By standardized he meant a very specific structure that was not to be broken. At first I thought he just meant I should try to standardize it, and the first time someone struggled with something I skipped it and moved on. I often did that, hoping that once they saw the big picture we could come back to the problem section and it would make more sense. If, for instance, someone struggled to understand the electronic timing system that ran the grill, I would skip that and come back to it later. After they saw the entire grill in operation through a lunch rush, the timing system made more sense. But when Mike found out I almost lost my position as a trainer. The timing system was to be covered first.

So I did what he wanted. It sucked. I think some of the people who completed the training did not really understand it all, but if the training sections could all be checked off, Mike didn't want to waste any more money on that and put them to work. If you have ever worked in a restaurant, you know it requires a lot of coordination among team members. Nothing is worse than working with people so poorly trained they can't pull their own weight. I still remember grill attendants who were so perplexed by the timing system that they never successfully mastered the other areas of the grill. Their worry about getting the timing system correct distracted them from understanding how it was really used.

In Mike's mind he was an excellent manager. He brought consistency to the training and that would improve the restaurant. But all he really did was make it difficult for people to get trained well. And that made it difficult for them to work well. Everybody's job was harder after three months with Mike.

Bad management can ruin a business. That doesn't always happen, though. Sometimes bad management keeps a company at a level of acceptable mediocrity so it simply never reaches its full potential. But bad management is a problem because of the negative effects it has on people, and it is at this level—the level of the individual, that the impact of business appears most powerful.

People are the heart and soul of business. Work and life don't balance, they just become more intertwined. If people are unhappy at work, there is a very good chance that it will carry over to the rest of their lives. Mihaly Csikszentmihalyi, famous for his research on the state of "flow," sums it up well (in *Good Business*):

> Our jobs determine to a large extent what our lives are like. Is what you do for a living making you ill? Does it keep you from becoming a more fully realized person? Do you feel ashamed of what you have to do at work? All too often, the answer to such questions is yes. Yet it does not have to be like that. Work can be one of the most joyful, most fulfilling aspects of life.

Most of the time people hate their jobs because of bad managers. By making the lives of their subordinates miserable, these managers are making the world worse off. I know I've fought with my wife about nothing just because I had a bad day at work and was in a grumpy mood. I'm sure many others have done the same thing. It works both ways, though. I've also come home with a huge grin on my face because I had a great day at work.

Why do work generated problems exist? If business has such significant effects on people, why can't they be positive? I think they can, but it takes a different mind-set. People who treat business as a paycheck producer rarely make great managers. People who treat business as something more can bring out the best in others.

My first job out of college was with a defense contractor. I designed computer chips for graphics processing. I got the chance to work on many different teams, with a vast cast of characters from the digital design department. It taught me the importance of working with people who can bring out the best in me.

For instance, I got a chance to work on a chip with a guy named Dave. He was known for being very, very, very laid back. He seemed so nonchalant about work that if you didn't know him, you would suspect he was a slacker who never got anything done.

But Dave was actually a very good designer. He hated to do extra work, so as a result he managed to pin down requirements early in the process. (For those of you who have never worked in a design related field, what typically happens is that the requirements keep changing right up until the design is released, making all the designers miserable and causing lots of unnecessary work.) Dave anticipated potential problems and was prepared when they arrived, and he managed upward as much as he managed downward. He let me attack problems in my own way, and he didn't micromanage. As long as my work got done, I was free to do my own thing. I liked working with Dave. I did my best work on that project. Our final review was the first in the history of the program to go through without a single recommended change. Chalk it up to the fact that we worked well together.

During that time I was happy and satisfied with my job. That translated over to my personal life too. That's why *Fast Company* was right when it launched in 1995 and declared that "work is personal." Work has a powerful effect on individuals. The managers I have worked for have brought out the good and the bad in me. You have the power to do the same in the people you manage. What you do matters. That is why business matters.

Business As The Neighborhood

I'm not sure when the neighborhood began to die. I grew up watching Andy Griffith and had the sense that not too long before my time, life had really been the way it was depicted on that show. They all knew their neighbors. Everyone knew everyone in

Mayberry. Was there really a time when life was about community?

My grandmother used to talk about a corner store. You know the kind, where the owner knows every customer and you run into your friends while shopping. You could actually run a tab because if you didn't pay, well, the owner knew where you lived. She told a lot of stories about things people used to do, back when neighborhoods meant something.

I can still see vestiges of those days here in Louisville. We have lots of neighborhoods, each with its own character. At one time, you went to school with your neighbors. Everyone supported local events because your neighborhood was your community.

But times change and people do too. We get busy. We get lost in TV shows, video games, surfing the Web, and all the stuff that has been made available to keep us occupied. It doesn't leave much time left for the community.

We are social beings and we need to spend time with other people. Isolation leads to bad things in humans. But that's what we have become—isolated. We are more connected than ever, yet we are still alone. It isn't that we can't talk to people, it's that we can't connect with people. Relationships take time to form and a two-minute cell phone call or a few hastily typed words in an instant message won't get it done. So how can we connect? Through work.

Business is the new neighborhood. It is the way we connect. Connection is about common ground and today that common ground isn't where you live, it's where you work. People are increasingly defined by the type of work they do and the companies they work for. Years ago you described yourself by where you lived and went to school, now it's by where you work and what you do.

The movement is most prominent among younger people. On the weekends they hang out with coworkers. If they need a referral for a service, they ask the people they work with because that is who they trust. I've known people to break a lawnmower and borrow one from a coworker on the other side of town instead of asking their next-door neighbor.

The last few years have seen a rise in social networking software. What do people use it for? Most use it to connect to people they want to work with, or previously worked with. I find that surprising. We don't use it to find romance, friends, or people with similar interests nearly as much as we use it to find people to work with. I think we don't always realize how much our work relationships mean to us. If business is our neighborhood, it's important that we like our neighbors.

The unique thing about business as a neighborhood is that unlike a geographic neighborhood, we get to screen our neighbors. It is important that we like the people we work with because we spend a great deal of time with them. To get things done, we have to support them and help them, and they have to support and help us. That is much easier when you like somebody. Screening applicants to see if they are a cultural fit allows companies to build their own cultures and communities. I once hired a guy who didn't fit in. I have this belief that managers should hire people who are different from them, but as I found out, that can be wrong. It all depends on what you mean by different.

Adam had a great résumé for someone his age. He said all the right things in the interview. He was quick-witted, extroverted, and very sociable. We were very different people and I thought he would pick up the slack where I failed. But it turned out that he was not a good fit. His style, mannerisms, and expectations—they were all very different from those of everyone else in the company. He was plenty nice, but he did not fit our community. Adam was like that neighbor that does something to his house. He likes it; everyone else thinks it's ugly. We could not understand each other. The tensions we sometimes experienced as a result manifested themselves as some tasks fell through the cracks.

Eventually, Adam had to go. He knew it and I knew it. He was not a good cultural fit. Diversity is good, and I still believe in hiring people who view the world and approach problems much differently than I do. But neighborhoods need some common bond to hold them together. Companies do, too. It is difficult to work with people who don't share a common basic view about the mission of a company.

The experience taught me that the state of a neighborhood depends on the people in it. In our business neighborhoods it is important to have a diversity of talent, skill, and interest, but we need common goals and mutual respect to hold it all together. We have to like our teammates and we have to feel like we have a valuable role to play within the team.

How To Make Business Matter

Community matters. Our neighborhoods matter, just as they always have. That is why business matters. Here's what to do about it:

See The Big Picture

In *The Essential Drucker*, Peter Drucker relays a favorite story from management meetings:

> Three stonecutters were asked what they were doing. The first replied "I am making a living." The second kept on hammering while he said "I am doing the best job of stonecutting in the entire county." The third one looked up with a visionary gleam in his eyes and said, "I am building a cathedral."

I've always viewed business like the third stonecutter. Maybe that's why I have such a hard time fitting into most modern organizations. I don't care about a job, I want more than that. Any time I am between projects or businesses, people always try to find me a job. They don't get it. They ask me, "What do you want to do?" But I never give an answer they expect. I don't want to manage. I don't want to program. I don't want to design products. I want to work toward a larger goal. If those things are steps along the way, then fine, I will do them; some of them I will even enjoy, but I do my best if I understand the greater goal.

Some people believe if you get all the little things right, the big things will take care of themselves. Other people believe that if you get all the big things right, the little things will take care of themselves. I don't know which is right, but I think in general, the big things are more difficult than the little things.

The big things are hard to see because little things cause all the fires that we have to put out. We become preoccupied with them. That's dangerous. It's like a basketball team that is more worried about executing the offense than winning the game. One may lead to another, but don't get so focused on the offense that you forget the larger goal.

The Reichstag in Berlin is a beautiful building, and like most structures built before the modern architectural era, it is very ornate. The detailed design of certain areas of the building is part of the reason people are attracted to it. But in 1995 two artists named Christo and Jean-Claude covered the entire Reichstag in fabric, hiding the details and exposing the essence of the structure. It was beautiful. The shape of the building, the larger form, had been ignored by people who were in awe of the decoration. With that decoration covered up, they could see and appreciate the beauty of the whole thing. I think many people in business today need to pull out some fabric and do the same thing.

When I ran a small business we had no customer service department, so every employee had to be trained to handle customer inquiries. My staff grew frustrated because I kept giving vague answers as to how to handle certain customer situations. It wasn't that I was avoiding an answer, I just didn't want the staff to use cookie-cutter approaches to answering customer questions and solving customer problems.

I resolved the issue by scheduling a meeting. I came into the room and passed out a sheet to each employee with a detailed set of instructions about how to behave when a customer entered the front door. They were relieved. It was exactly what they wanted. Then I asked them to crumple up the paper and throw it in the garbage. They thought it was a joke so I repeated myself. With confused looks on their faces, they complied.

We walked outside the building and I made them go in one by one and take note of their first impression. After that we had a discussion about higher-level goals. We wanted customers to have a great experience no matter what it took. I explained that rules and guidelines might be helpful, but I didn't want anyone to hide behind them. Solve the problem. Meet the need. See the bigger picture. They finally began to understand.

We forget that business matters when we get so concerned about the little things that we forget the larger impact. We forget that everything we do and say makes a difference. We forget that great companies can change the world and that poor companies can drag it down. We forget that the performance of a team has a lot to do with the situation and with the relationships of those involved. When we take a step back we remember what is really important.

Make It Personal

I've been a Meg Ryan fan for as long as I can remember, and one of my favorite movies is *You've Got Mail*. Most people don't realize how much that movie is about business. Ryan plays Kathleen Kelly, the owner of a small bookstore that is eventually put out of business by Fox Books, a superchain run by Tom Hanks's character, Joe Fox. In one scene in the movie, Fox tells Kelly that putting her out of business "wasn't personal." She responds by asking what that means. "After all," she says, "if business is anything, shouldn't it be personal?"

Why do we try so hard to separate our business and personal lives? Do we hate work that much? Are we just trying to do the minimum it takes to get by? If so, what's the point? If business can make such an impact on the world, why don't we take our business more seriously?

My dad used to be director of engineering at the Louisville airport. He's been off doing other things for more than ten years, but he basically supervised the construction of the new terminal back in the mid-1980s. Several months ago he took me to the airport and as we drove up a ramp to the passenger departure area, he noticed a large crack in the concrete. He slowed down and stared at it. "That shouldn't have happened yet," he said. "That concrete isn't even twenty years old." I wondered why he cared. He said, "I feel bad." I laughed, but you have to understand, work is very personal to him. He loves to build things and he takes it personally when they don't turn out right.

Making it personal changes everything. If it is personal, it becomes more than a job. We come to feel as if our work says something about who we are. It isn't just something we do for a paycheck, it's an expression of our skills and abilities. As the old saying goes, "Every job is a self-portrait of those who did it. Autograph your work with quality." It's true—and difficult to do without taking your job personally. If business matters, and we take our business personally, good things will happen.

Why do we try so hard to separate our business and personal lives? Do we hate work that much?

Harness The Power

Some people who want to change the world are anti-business. They blame businesses for the problems they see, and they think the answer is to shut them down, regulate them, or let the government run them. But it's not. Businesses are complex systems and such simple answers won't work. These people tend to use protests and advertising campaigns to raise awareness of the issues. They should try harnessing the power of business instead.

Instead of complaining about the way a certain company treats the environment, why not find a way to solve its waste problem in a profitable way? Win-win solutions are out there, but they take hard work and creativity to find.

Whatever your passions, whatever problems you see, whatever needs aren't being met, those are business opportunities. People often talk about wanting to do noble things like join the Peace Corps, help the homeless, reduce poverty, and save the environment. That is great, but if you want to change the world–start a business. Reduce poverty by employing more people. Help the homeless by designing affordable and functional housing. Improve the environment by helping companies recycle, reduce waste, and conserve energy in a way that translates to their bottom line. It can be done, but it takes people who understand and embrace the power of business to do so.

Ultimately, business is all about human beings–our needs, our wants, and our desires. It is nothing but a vehicle for harnessing our collective power to achieve our goals. Like any other tool, it isn't good or bad in and of itself–the way we use it is what is important. In that way, business is a reflection of us. It matters because we matter. We all work, but do we all embrace our work to make a difference?

> Ultimately, business is all about human beings—our needs, our wants, and our desires. It is nothing but a vehicle for harnessing our collective power to achieve our goals.

FROM THE EDITOR

BusinessPundit.com was one of the first business blogs I came across, and it's what got me to start my own blog (www.apennyfor.com). Rob was doing the same thing I wanted to do–posting links to interesting articles in the business media. He even started blogging for the same reason I did—to give his wife relief from his constant business commentary. You will find him living by Churchill Downs tinkering with all sorts of ideas these days.

In His Own Words . . .

What is it about your essay topic that made you want to write this chapter in *More Space*?

"Because it aggravates me that people don't want to engage in a discussion about a topic that affects so many areas of their lives."

Rob's blog:
www.businesspundit.com

Rob's favorite blogs:
bigpicture.typepad.com
www.mindhacks.com
www.corante.com/brainwaves

Recommended reading:
Good Business
by Mihaly Csikszentmihalyi
Re-imagine!
by Tom Peters
Any books by Peter Drucker

Work Is Broken—Here's How We Fix It

by Marc Orchant

Let me tell you about Bill.

Years ago, I worked with a charming and ambitious fellow. Let's call him Bill. You probably know a lot of people who have worked with someone just like Bill. Maybe you have.

Bill was always ready with an informed opinion. He had the latest industry information at his fingertips and knew exactly who was in what deal and who was jockeying for which position both in our company and at every competitor.

Bill could rattle off every call and site visit he'd made and comment on every sales proposal we had under consideration. He had the facts . . . he had the figures.

Bill could do a PowerPoint presentation at the drop of a hat. He practiced hard and mastered his script. He was smooth, professional, and polished.

Bill would boast about the number of e-mails he received and how full of important correspondence his Inbox was at all times.

He would proudly show you his schedule on his Palm Pilot to demonstrate how he managed to pack more into every day than most people could ever imagine attempting.

Sounds great, right? Sounds like every organization, even yours, could use a few more Bills, huh?

I wouldn't wish Bill on my worst enemy.

How's that? Excuse, me? What'd you just say?

Isn't Bill a shining example of all that we should try to be? Polished? Smooth? Well-connected? On the ball? A master of efficiency and productivity?

Bill was a train wreck. Bill left a wake of unhappy people behind him wherever he went.

Let me explain.

Bill's ability to reconstruct every call and site visit he'd made was a one-dimensional parlor trick. He could tell you where he'd been and with whom he'd met in perfect detail. But when it came to sharing any substance about the "what"—what was discussed, what next steps were required to close the deal, what our team in the field needed—Bill wasn't nearly as accurate or detailed. He wanted you to be impressed by how much he'd done, not how well he'd done it.

Bill's presentation might have been polished but it was devoid of any real meaning. Despite the opportunity to engage or teach his audience, he instead chose to parrot facts and figures. His job was supposed to be helping prospects and customers understand the challenges and opportunities they could expect if they entered the market we were developing. Instead, he told the same old story over and over about how one company had done something completely unrelated to the audience's business and it was impossible to reproduce. Of course, this carefully scripted one-way mirror was precisely rendered in classic "three bullet points to a slide" style.

Great story—no takeaway.

Sending Bill e-mail was an exercise in frustration. It was like a black hole—everything went in but nothing came out. Bill would process all of his mail in batches every day or two and then reply as he saw fit. Often, he'd call and a leave a hasty voice mail message in response to a request for some detailed information. In the voice mail, he'd usually tell you who else you might want to check with for that information—Bill was busy.

And it was hard to predict what he might respond to, in what order, and when. On a number of occasions, I had requested some time-sensitive information from Bill and the only e-mail I got from him was about industry gossip or forwarded joke-mail. He seemed to have no sense of how to prioritize his mail and no appreciation of business etiquette.

Bill's schedule was a marvel. He'd mastered airline ticketing, airport logistics, and the car rental game. He knew how to get in and out of a city better than anyone I'd ever met. Bill would neatly dovetail meetings to maximize his efficiency but left no room for error and no allowance for opportunity. When it was time to go to his next appointment he just got up and left. Whoever else from our company was in the meeting was left to "finish up," as Bill called it—meaning salvage whatever was possible of the original mission.

To make sure he accomplished what he wanted in these meetings, he'd ignore any agenda or scripting his team tried to prepare and discuss in advance. Bill prided himself on his skill at taking over any meeting and winging it.

Bill was the poster child for just about every symptom of what's broken in the world of work for so many:

- Shallow, superficial communications
- No follow-through on commitments
- Misplaced priorities
- No long-term planning—everything done on the fly, at the last minute

It's Not Just The Corporate World That's Broken

I've spent most of my professional life working for and building small companies. The corporate experience I just wrote about was an aberration in my life. As with most people, my work experience has been primarily in what analysts call "small" business (250 employees or less). And, surely, smaller organizations should be better at weeding out the Bills of this world, right? In a smaller company, people can't get away with that stuff. Everyone knows everyone else and there's greater accountability.

Sorry to be the one that bursts your bubble. It turns out that there's a magic number for how many employees a company can have and be confident of providing that utopian work environment. And it's not the analysts' cut-off for "small" business. It's not even fifty people. It's two.

Hear me out.

You have to have two people to have communication. It takes two people to have a phone conversation, a meeting, or to exchange e-mail. You can't delegate a task unless at least one other person is involved. Even doing a little celebratory high-five after receiving some good news ("We got the Wilson contract!") works best if you have someone to slap palms with.

OK . . . so two is the minimum. But it's also the maximum if you want 100 percent certainty that everyone is accountable and on the same page. Because as soon as you add one more, the possibility of two people meeting without the third becomes a reality. And a lot of broken communication arises when we fail to accurately capture and share what transpired in a meeting with those who weren't there.

Look—it's hard enough to get complete agreement between two people on many subjects. Ask anyone who's married or been in a committed relationship (and yes, that does include business partners). The potential for misunderstanding, misinterpretation, misrepresentation, and a host of other "mis-es" rises exponentially as you add more people to the equation.

So just because you work for a small company, nonprofit organization, or educational institution, don't get comfortable. Work is still broken.

WHY WORK IS BROKEN

The nature of work has been undergoing profound change, and many of the practices employed by individuals, teams, and companies have not kept up with these changes. Tom Peters's most recent work, *Re-imagine!*, is a tour de force of reflection on this very topic. In his own inimitable fashion, Peters rants and raves about many of the changes we're experiencing and suggests that if you fail to acknowledge, prepare for, and react to these changes, you are destined to be left scratching your head wondering "What happened?" Some of the changes to watch for:

- Outsourcing
- The death of the manufacturing economy (in the West)
- The rise of the Hispanic and women's population in both the consumer market and world of business
- The importance of design and "wow" in creating new markets
- "Always-on" communications and real-time information access

Peters is a big thinker and he tackles big issues. I'm concerned here with issues on a smaller scale. But the implications for your work are no less profound and will affect you every bit as much as the megatrends Peters has been discussing of late.

Consider how your work life has been transformed in the last few years. Think about how frequently you use a fax machine these days. A few years back, faxes and overnight packages were the primary means of exchanging documents. Today, ubiquitous and cheap broadband, broad adoption of PDF for document exchange, voice (and video) over IP, and other technologies have fundamentally changed the way we interact with our coworkers, suppliers, partners, and customers. Blogs, podcasts, wikis, and streaming video from the desktop have virtualized meetings, conversations, and other information exchanges in ways we only recently considered to be in the realm of science fiction.

Question: How different from the *Star Trek* communicator are the advanced cell phones we're using today?

The essential nature of work has undergone similar transformation for many people, especially those of us engaged in "knowledge work." Back when I worked with Bill, I was part of a well-defined team of people. I knew my role and how and where I fit into the ecosystem. I had a discrete set of responsibilities and a clearly defined area of authority.

Today, by contrast, I'm involved in many projects. My role in each varies and is subject to change over the life of that effort. I may be a manager, a team member, an initiator, or a resource. I lead some projects and play only a bit part in others. I may be involved

[Tom] Peters is a big thinker and he tackles big issues. I'm concerned here with issues on a smaller scale. But the implications for your work are no less profound and will affect you every bit as much as the megatrends Peters has been discussing of late.

in a particular initiative from the very first brainstorming session and only asked to help out with another as it nears completion. And all this happens on a daily basis with an ebb and flow that is sometimes as predictable as the tides and at other times as surprising as one of the flash floods we see here in the desert southwest after a mountain storm.

Question: How many different roles do you have in your work today? How does this compare with your work five years ago? Ten years ago?

Because we have so many ways to interact, it has become all too easy to fall prey to a kind of information overload our parents (and even older siblings) could never have imagined. It's become a cliché that our lives are much more complex and immediate than the way things were in the "good old days." But, as with most truisms, there's substance behind those familiar words. This complexity has shattered many of the conventions and techniques we've grown accustomed to relying on to do our work.

THINGS THAT HAVE BROKEN

Meetings, presentations, and e-mails are a part of many people's workday. Used effectively, each can help keep teams aligned, impart important information, and move projects forward. In addition to the paper we've been trained to work with since our earliest school days, we now are bombarded with information from the Web, blogs, wikis, intranets, search engines, and other digital sources. We're challenged to develop and maintain a system for collecting, processing, and acting on all this information we receive as never before. And the classic techniques we've relied on in the past have either ceased to be effective or have simply broken. The current state of affairs in many people's daily existence is a succession of mind-numbing meetings, uninformative presentations, and chaotic (often unmanageable) e-mail and analog Inboxes with hundreds of unread, unprocessed, and unfiled messages, articles, and reports.

Meetings have become the bane of many an office worker's existence. Many people have "serial meeting days" where they seem to do nothing except attend meetings. Almost universally, those days leave people feeling as though they have accomplished little or nothing. How often have you heard someone say, "I got nothing done today; I spent my entire day in meetings."

Too many meetings have little or no structure, poorly formulated agendas, and unclear roles for the participants. With attendees unsure of what goals the meeting is intended to accomplish and lacking a well-articulated structure, meetings often descend into an anarchic free-for-all that tends to be dominated by a few strong personalities. By contrast, a well-designed meeting can be a profoundly productive experience that energizes a project team, produces a coherent vision, and generates concrete actions that move a project forward.

Unfortunately, too many meetings become an excuse to subject attendees to what is often described as "Death by PowerPoint." Few experiences are more depressing than attending a meeting in which you watch the back of someone's head as they read their PowerPoint slides verbatim, as if everyone else in the room has lost the capacity to read. This phenomenon unfortunately extends to conferences, seminars, and training sessions. The art of delivering effective presentations may not be dying, but it surely seems to be in increasingly short supply where we work.

The old saying—"It's a poor craftsman who blames his tools"—does apply to those who use PowerPoint presentations as a crutch to support a meeting that lacks a clear purpose or agenda. I've witnessed some absolutely dreadful presentations. But I've also seen masterful use of the tool where it informs, illuminates, and expands on the

Too many meetings have little or no structure, poorly formulated agendas, and unclear roles for the participants. With attendees unsure of what goals the meeting is intended to accomplish and lacking a well-articulated structure, meetings often descend into an anarchic free-for-all that tends to be dominated by a few strong personalities. By contrast, a well-designed meeting can be a profoundly productive experience that energizes a project team, produces a coherent vision, and generates concrete actions that move a project forward.

speaker's verbal presentation. Used appropriately, a PowerPoint presentation can add tremendous value to a meeting.

The final entry on my list of things that have broken is e-mail. Many people have become victims of what I call the "incredible exploding Inbox." Between spam, sheer inundation, and poor e-mail etiquette, what was once a vital and near real-time communication tool has become a morass. It's been estimated that as much as 80 percent of what finds its way into most people's e-mail Inboxes ends up being deleted almost immediately. And what's left, once the unreadable foreign-character gibberish and obvious spam has been eliminated, is poorly formatted and difficult to respond to or act on.

Many e-mails these days have a subject line that contains multiple instances of FW:, RE:, and other junk that obscures the meaning behind the message. Have you received a message with a subject line like this lately?

FW: FW: RE: Your last message regarding. . . .

Question: What are you supposed to make of that? Is this likely to be the first e-mail you want to read in your crowded Inbox? Even if it's from your boss?

Effective e-mail triage depends on the ability to quickly get the gist of a message so that good decisions can be made about what to read and respond to first. Indecipherable subject lines, as big a problem as they are, represent only the first obstacle in using e-mail effectively. Even when you've opened many of the e-mail messages you receive, you're often faced with hunting your way through quoted message text, sometimes two or three levels deep, before you can find the part of the message that needs your action.

And the problem doesn't even end there. E-mail overload has created a peculiar loss of reason that leads otherwise intelligent and reasonable people to do something completely irrational:

They keep everything in their Inbox!

This makes no sense at all. Oh, I do understand the rationale behind this behavior. Here's a little quiz. Answer honestly—only you will know the answers you provide. Have you ever used any of the following excuses to justify having hundreds or thousands of e-mails in your Inbox?

1. If I file this away somewhere, I'll forget about it.
2. There might be something important in this e-mail.
3. I'll get to this as soon as I catch up on some other stuff that's more important.
4. I really need to have this right in front of me.
5. If I keep this marked as unread I'll know it's something I need to act on.

Does this sound familiar? Looking at it objectively, doesn't this sound a little crazy?

E-mail can be an effective tool and it is increasingly the single biggest source of what David Allen, author of *Getting Things Done*, calls "next actions." As I begin discussing solutions, I'll show you how to streamline your e-mail processing, extract the next actions each message contains, and file and store your mail so you will be able to find information when you need it. The ultimate goal, as Allen puts it, is to "get In to empty" (repeat that out loud—you'll get it) and achieve a Zen-like state he refers to as "mind like water."

Note: This phrase comes from an old martial arts teaching. The master asks, "How does the water in a pond respond when a pebble is tossed into it?" After the student shrugs, unable to answer, the master imparts the following wisdom, "Appropriately. The pebble

> It's been estimated that as much as 80 percent of what finds its way into most people's e-mail Inboxes ends up being deleted almost immediately.

displaces the water, causing ripples which radiate outward. The water then returns to its normal state—smooth as glass, undisturbed and prepared for the next pebble."

The lesson is to respond appropriately to whatever task or event you're currently occupied with—don't overreact or underreact. After you have responded, return to a natural state of ready repose.

Ways To Fix What's Broken

We have three ways to deal with information overload. We can choose to be like my old coworker Bill and slough it off—bouncing from one engagement to the next leaving a wake of destruction behind. That's a lot harder to get away with these days. Because we are responsible to so many people in an interconnected web of projects and because instant communication has become the norm, people like Bill can't really get away with skipping stone-like across the surface for very long. So scratch irresponsibility and a cavalier attitude off the list of successful strategies.

We can scale back. Commit to less. Focus on what's important to us and stop trying to do everything. Bill Jensen, author of *The Simplicity Survival Handbook* and *Work 2.0*, is an authority on how to create less stress by letting go and learning that it's OK to say no a lot more often that you might think. I encourage you to look at some of his ideas and techniques. He's a really smart, funny guy who has put a lot of effort into researching, quantifying, and developing strategies to address what's broken about work. Here are a few choice observations from "Ten Simple Truths," a chapter in *The Simplicity Survival Handbook*:

- In most of today's workplaces, Work = Figuring out what to do with finite time and attention, and infinite information and choices.

- R-E-S-P-E-C-T now includes how well, or poorly, your company, your manager, and your teammates use the finite time you have available every day (and how well, or poorly, you use theirs!).

- Plan and manage change all you want. Just know that execution travels at the speed of sense-making. Create less clutter and more clarity, or help everyone make sense of it faster than the competition, and you win.

Jensen's Simplicity approach is a good start. Certainly committing to less makes keeping the commitments you do make easier and more likely to happen. But learning to say no isn't a solution—it's only a strategy. Even if you've managed to cut down on the common practice of taking on too much, you'll still find you have a lot to do and will need an approach to manage and execute on the many tasks you're charged with.

The third strategy is to impose order on chaos. A seemingly endless supply of books, tapes, and analog and electronic tools promise to help us get and stay organized, be more effective and productive, make our whites whiter and our breath fresher. The productivity business is a multimillion-dollar enterprise that enriches the people who sell the stuff a whole lot more than those of us who buy it. It's easy to feel frustrated and to assume that some fundamental flaw in us prevents us from succeeding with these fabulous inventions. Take heart. Despite the old saying, sometimes it is the tools that make the difference. Some processes and tools really can help you get a handle on your information overload.

A New Approach To Fixing What's Broken

Over the last four years, I've been part of a team that has developed a new approach to work. Our approach addresses every one of these broken processes. We've combined elements from a number of productivity gurus' teachings, some bits of low- and high-tech gear, and a participatory process to achieve a level of productivity, ownership, and satisfaction with work I've never experienced before. Stress levels are low, morale is high, and results are measurable and sustained.

One of the reasons our approach to fixing work has succeeded is because everyone has the opportunity to participate in the development, implementation, and constant improvement of the process. Because no one person owns it, everyone can take ownership in it.

I know this sounds pretty far-fetched if you're stuck in a toxic workplace, but it accurately describes the workplace I go to every day. And you can apply every one of these ideas to your work—the only variable is how you will apply them. You may use these techniques personally, within your work group or project team, or introduce them into your entire organization.

FIXING MEETINGS

Imagine looking forward to a meeting with the expectation that you will leave with a clear sense of what you need to do, by when, and for whom, as well as what you can expect to get from your team members. Further, imagine having a clear idea of the role you're expected to play in the meeting, having access to appropriate materials, and a reasonable amount of time to prepare any advance work you might need to bring to the meeting.

There's nothing magic about making meetings like this the norm at your workplace. As Bill Jensen says, it's a question of R-E-S-P-E-C-T. You need a process that is clearly defined, well documented, endorsed by management, and publicly agreed to by all participants. Behold the power of peer pressure!

Here are some of the tools we use to ensure every meeting is a positive and productive experience.

Invitations That Create Anticipation, Not Avoidance

Meeting invitations should make all participants (and stakeholders not in attendance) aware of what the purpose and end product of that gathering will be. Whether you use a paper memo, calendaring program, or a group e-mail, great meetings start with a well-crafted invitation. State a specific objective for the meeting and the activities you will conduct to achieve that objective. Be sure to provide some context for the end product of this meeting. It might read something like this:

> In this meeting, we will brainstorm ideas for our next white paper using an affinity session. We will generate a short list of topics (2–3) that will be handed off to marketing to develop into abstracts. With those abstracts, we will reconvene and select our next white paper. Please review our "Paper Products Workflow" guide, available on the intranet, prior to the meeting.

Every meeting invitation should include a brief agenda and identify who will own critical roles like discussion leader, scribe, and timekeeper. If the structure of the meeting is clearly spelled out and the invitation is sent far enough in advance to allow time for preparation, everyone participating will have all the information they need to show up ready to accomplish the meeting's goals. They'll arrive with a clear idea of what they're expected to contribute to and take away from the meeting. The roles I just mentioned are critical to every meeting. Depending on the nature of the meeting, the group may need others.

The agenda need not be overly elaborate—shorter is definitely better. For our brain-storming meeting (a one-hour affair), the invitation would include an agenda and role assignment list like this:

Location: Upstairs Conference Room

Time: 10:00–11:00 A.M.

Agenda:

- 10:00–10:15 A.M.: Review the objectives for our white papers
- 10:15–10:45 A.M.: Affinity brainstorming
- 10:45–11:00 A.M.: Assign next actions

Roles:

- Discussion leader: Marc
- Scribe: Joan
- Timekeeper: Bob
- Other attendees: Jim, Casey, Mike, Molly

I'm sure you can appreciate the value in getting a meeting invitation like this, and I hope you can see that it isn't a particularly difficult or time-consuming thing to do. The first person to start issuing invitations like this will undoubtedly hear a few kind words of appreciation from one or more of the attendees—along these lines: "Thanks, Lee. I always appreciate how organized your meetings are. I really feel good about what we accomplished here today."

That's a nice thing and certainly doesn't hurt your reputation among your peers as an efficient, respectful, and well-organized individual. People will be happy to attend your meetings because they will rapidly develop an expectation that your meetings produce results.

When everyone in an organization does this, meetings are transformed from soul-sucking black holes into something people can look forward to.

Contract For Communications

For procedures like this to take hold and become institutionalized, everyone in the organization needs to be on the same page. One of the most powerful tools we've developed is a company-wide "Contract for Communications." This document was drafted by a team of people from every department and at every level of our company. Comments were solicited and changes made until we had broad consensus that we had crafted a clear statement of how we wanted to communicate with each other. Now every employee receives a copy of this contract and signs it.

This contract describes rules of engagement, meeting processes, e-mail etiquette, and even voice mail procedures. I've included a digest of our contract in this chapter's appendix for you to review and potentially use as a starting point for your own work group, department, or organization.

Tips For More Engaging And Effective Meetings

Affinity is a brainstorming technique using standard, inexpensive office supplies that encourages a group of people to generate an amazing quantity of raw ideas, provides a means for them to organize and label them, and uses the "wisdom of crowds" principle to condense the results into a list of the best and most readily implemented ideas.

Here's how it works:

1. Every meeting participant gets a Post-it notepad (3" square is a good size) and a broad-tip marker (Sharpies work well) for writing on them.

2. Write a single question on the whiteboard or easel pad in your meeting room. *Brainstorm one question at a time.* For our white paper brainstorming session, for example, my group would write the following question on our whiteboard: What topics might we develop into our next white paper?

3. Everyone works independently and jots down as many ideas as they can. Emphasize quantity over quality at this stage of the exercise. The more ideas you end up with, the better the next steps will work. Tell everyone how long this part of the exercise will last. Typically, we spend no more than ten minutes generating ideas.

4. At the end of the generation period (remember to assign someone the timekeeper role), everyone gathers their notes and sticks them to the whiteboard or easel pad. After all the notes have been placed, each participant takes a few minutes (two or three minutes is usually sufficient) to read everyone else's ideas.

5. If someone has written an idea that creates a "light bulb moment," anyone should feel free to jot down another idea or two and add it to the collection. Encourage this—some of the best ideas I've seen generated come from this second round.

6. Everyone now begins a clustering process, picking up related ideas and grouping them together. This is critical: *everyone assists with the clustering process*. Get people out of their chairs. You will not believe how much of a difference this group activity can make in your meetings. Leave some room around each grouping to add a label for that set of ideas and to jot down additional notes. Duplicates should be stuck on top of each other, not discarded. If two or three people have the same idea, that's often an indication that this is an idea you should look at closely.

7. Discuss the clusters. Jot down the positives and negatives of each cluster of ideas (remember to assign someone the scribe role) as it is discussed by the group. These notes can be written directly on the whiteboard but I've found it's better to create a new note (or two) with this analysis.

8. Depending on the outcome you defined in the agenda, conduct a vote or perform a winnowing process verbally to shorten the list to meet your stated objective. In this example, the goal was to narrow the list down to two or three options.

9. Have the scribe gather all of the ideas and analysis notes for transcription into a report that should be distributed to all meeting attendees (and stakeholders not in attendance). We sometimes use a digital camera to photograph the board before taking down the notes and use that as a reference for creating the meeting report. If your meeting produces actions and assignments, share them with all attendees and stakeholders as soon after the meeting as possible.

Mind Maps

Mind mapping is a dynamic and fluid brainstorming and capture technique that can be used to engage even the most reticent meeting attendee in the process of visualizing ideas and project plans. Mind maps are technology-independent; you can create them

Mind mapping is a dynamic and fluid brainstorming and capture technique that can be used to engage even the most reticent meeting attendee in the process of visualizing ideas and project plans.

on an easel pad, a whiteboard, or on a PC attached to a digital projector. For software, I am a big fan of Mindjet's MindManager X5—but a number of other good applications are available for Windows, Macintosh, and Linux.

The essence of mind mapping as a meeting tool is similar to affinity but is conducted interactively with the entire group. You start with a central element that contains the question you wish to brainstorm. Then begin a discussion of broad topical areas, each of which is added to a branch radiating from the central element. After you've exhausted that level of discussion (set a time limit—it keeps the discussion moving when everyone is on the clock) move to more specific ideas under each broad category.

After the idea generation phase, it's a simple matter to drag ideas from one branch to another as necessary, adding notes and even icons and other graphics. You can also link reference documents and Web pages to branch items.

Mind mapping encourages meeting participants to build on each other's thoughts and suggestions and produces an organic display of the group's creative process that literally grows before everyone's eyes, producing a diagram like the one in Figure 1. I've used this technique for years and have never grown tired of it. In our organization, a number of people have MindManager installed on their laptop or desktop PCs. Distributing the map is easy—you can send the native map file or generate a Word outline, PowerPoint slide deck, or PDF file from MindManager. You can even generate HTML pages that can be posted to your intranet.

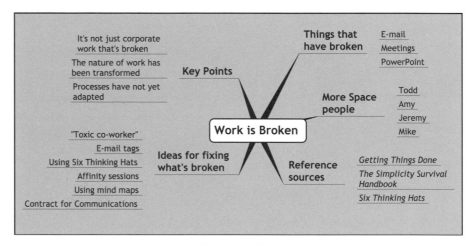

Figure 1. Mind Map

Six Thinking Hats

Edward de Bono's *Six Thinking Hats* process defines a way to make meetings safe, egoless, and more effective by creating a shared understanding of what voice the group is using at any given point in a meeting. It's a powerful way to give everyone an effective voice in group discussions. Wearing a *Green hat* means the group is in creative mode, generating ideas but not analyzing them. *White hat* time is used to define what information is on hand and what is needed. *Red hat* time allows each participant to share personal thoughts about the idea or project being discussed with no need to justify these feelings or defend them. *Black hat* time is for exploring the logical negatives associated with an idea or topic, while *Yellow hat* time focuses on the logical positives. *Blue hat* time is reserved for meeting logistics and management.

A key element in a *Six Thinking Hats* meeting is sequencing the hats. This can be done in advance (in which case it can be included in the meeting invitation and agenda) or at the beginning of the meeting. There is a real art to sequencing a meeting—it's a lot harder than it sounds. While *Six Thinking Hats* is a great technique, it's only worthwhile if everyone understands how the process works. We sent everyone in our company to a full-day training session with a certified de Bono trainer. A less expensive approach is to buy everyone a copy of the book and develop some internal training and practice sessions. We don't use hats on an everyday basis, but when we do, it's effective. I've found it especially useful for large meetings or those dealing with hot topics where emotions may run high.

Six Thinking Hats has helped with everyday meetings and even conversations, because it has become part of our shared vocabulary. It's not unusual to hear someone say "OK, I'm just green hatting here, but it seems to me—". The context this provides for the points being made during a discussion removes ambiguity and lets the other people involved in the conversation know precisely what perspective the speaker is coming from.

We recently had an engagement with a consultant who was unfamiliar with *Six Thinking Hats*. We provided her with a brief explanation of each hat so she could interact with our team with a clear understanding of how we were talking about what we were talking about. By the end of the second day, she was referencing the hats (especially red and white hats) as comfortably as any of us. Using the *Six Thinking Hats* helped us cut through a bit of tension early on in the first day of our meetings with the consultant and allowed us to communicate much more effectively.

FIXING PRESENTATIONS: THE POWERPOINT PROBLEM

PowerPoint, when used inappropriately, can actually stupefy meetings, not make them smarter. The constraints of a presentation format make it difficult to create the kind of dynamic environment that meetings should provide but often fail to deliver. Creative strategies for conducting effective meetings may use some of the techniques described in this chapter to engage participants in conversation and an exchange of ideas. A content-heavy PowerPoint presentation, on the other hand, can turn a meeting into a one-sided lecture that generally fails to produce meaningful results or tasks capable of moving a project forward.

Instead of subjecting the attendees at your next meeting to yet another endless litany of bullet points, consider using PowerPoint as a means to display the agenda for the meeting and nothing more. Tom Peters has become famous for one-slide PowerPoint presentations—sometimes with only a single word or question showing for the entire speech. Watch Steve Jobs at MacWorld to see how he uses Keynote to provide title slides that describe in a word or two what he's currently discussing. Adapt those public speaking techniques for your meetings. Never read your PowerPoint slides. They should only provide a summary of the points you plan to talk about.

Move Beyond Bullet Points

Any number of books and an equal or greater number of blogs talk about ways to use PowerPoint more effectively. Many of these resources, while well-intentioned, fail to do more than provide design tips and techniques on how to use transitions and other multimedia features in the program. I don't know about you, but if I sit through another PowerPoint presentation that uses that stupid typewriter sound effect I'll probably lose my mind.

One of the truly original thinkers in the world of PowerPoint and the art of presentations is Cliff Atkinson of Sociable Media. Cliff has a great blog called "Beyond Bullets" and is the author of a new book (out in March 2005) titled *Beyond Bullet Points*. It will help you rethink your approach not just to PowerPoint but to the art of presentation making. What Cliff counsels is a complete revamping of the way you approach putting together a presentation.

Cliff teaches a three-step process for constructing a presentation that reverses what almost everyone does when creating a presentation. Think about how you usually approach creating a new PowerPoint presentation. You probably launch PowerPoint and start typing. Right? According to Cliff, this is exactly backwards from what you should be doing. Instead, think about creating your presentation in much the same way a movie is produced. Start with a script (your story), then develop a storyboard to design the visual flow of your presentation, and then (and only then) start building the presentation.

Consider this quote from the introduction to *Beyond Bullet Points*:

> But although bullet points make it easy for us to create slides, they don't always make it easy for audiences to understand what we want to say. Growing numbers of people are expressing a sense of frustration with the conventional bullet points approach, and they're expressing themselves in a wide range of forums including discussion groups, surveys, books, essays, articles and blog postings. What they're saying, basically, is that slides filled with bullet points create obstacles between presenters and audiences. You might want to be natural and relaxed when you present, but people say that bullet points make the atmosphere formal and stiff. You might aim to be clear and concise, but people often walk away from these presentations feeling confused and unclear. And you might intend to display the best of your critical thinking on a screen, but people say that bullet points "dumb down" the important discourse that needs to happen for our society to function well.

The *Beyond Bullet Points* Web site offers a number of free downloads I encourage you to look at— http://www.sociablemedia.com/thebook_resources.php4. You can download a PDF of the table of contents, the introduction (from which this quote was taken), and the first chapter of the book as well as numerous templates to help you generate your script and storyboard your presentation.

Fixing E-mail

Fixing e-mail is a complex problem because it's broken in a number of ways. Poorly constructed subject lines are the first problem. Badly formatted messages are the second. And the sheer volume of mail many knowledge workers have to process every day is the third problem. As with meetings, the solutions we've implemented at my company blend the great ideas we've learned from really smart people and some good stuff we've cooked up for ourselves.

Fixing The Subject Line

As we wrestled with the problem of how to make e-mail more effective, it became apparent the first thing we needed was a way to make the subject line more useful. An e-mail subject line should provide some immediate information to help the recipient prioritize new mail. We developed a series of easy-to-remember tags that begin the subject line in all our internal e-mail to accomplish this with just two or three letters.

The change this has made in how we all process and respond to e-mail has been nothing short of miraculous. Response times for urgent requests have been trimmed from hours to minutes for those messages that require immediate attention. Less important items are easy to spot and can easily be filed for reference or action at a later date.

Our company runs on e-mail. With these tags and some of the techniques that follow, empty Inboxes are a regular occurrence, even for those of us who receive hundreds of messages every day. I have three very active e-mail addresses and regularly receive 150–250 messages a day. Yet I have a completely empty Inbox at least three times a week and always leave the office on Friday with every piece of mail processed and acted upon.

Here are the tags we've developed:

- RR: Reply requested
- RRAL: Reply Requested At Leisure
- URG: Urgent
- NRN: No Reply Necessary
- RAL: Read At Leisure
- IMP: Important (but not requiring action)
- INT: Internal (generally used for policy or procedure announcements)
- SAI: Strategic Awareness Info (industry news—read as time permits)
- FYI: For Your Information (no action required)

Some sample e-mail subject lines:

RR: Please review these updated Web pages

RRAL: Follow-up on your research request

URG: This bug may be a show stopper—status?

INT: Our new travel procedure

FYI: Server maintenance scheduled for this evening

SAI: Symantec makes another acquisition

Each of these subject lines contains all the information I need to make a quick decision about what to do. The URG message gets opened right away, of course. The RR message concerning new Web pages will be read promptly as it probably contains a due date for feedback. The other advantage these tags provide is that if I sort my Inbox by Subject, all similarly tagged messages are immediately grouped together. It's a low-tech but very useful solution.

Fixing The Message Body

As e-mail threads grow, formatting issues begin to crop up that can make it difficult to find the fresh information in the latest message in a conversation. Because of the volume of mail we generate, and because a lot of the developers on staff read their mail in a terminal window, we avoid using HTML for internal mail. Text-only mail has a more consistent appearance in different reading environments, is more compact, and is easier to copy and paste. There *are* a lot of good uses for HTML e-mail. What I'm talking about here is internal business communications at a software company.

More important than the actual file format is what you put into your e-mail . . . or rather, what you *don't*. Most e-mail clients quote all the previous text in a conversation thread. You can turn this feature off but most people don't. As a result, I (you, we) get messages that are a mile long containing our own message text, everyone else's message text, and quotes and requotes, ad infinitum. It's like walking through a house of mirrors!

Here's a simple solution for internal e-mail: be deliberate about using quoting. And, while you're at it, turn off automatic e-mail signatures too. Use the "reply with quote" feature (or copy and paste) when it is appropriate to quote a previous message but don't do it reflexively. If you have a well-crafted subject line (see above) and a well-written message body, your coworkers will know what you're writing about. They don't need their own message parroted back to them. And they don't need the clutter of everyone's signature in the message as well—sometimes two or more times.

External e-mail is another thing entirely. I'm certainly not advocating you never use quoting or include the entire message thread. There are obvious cases, like introducing a new person into an ongoing conversation, where providing the narrative for what has already been discussed has enormous value.

FIXING THE INBOX—HOW TO DEAL WITH E-MAIL OVERLOAD

This is a big topic. Entire books have been written about how to deal with the insane volumes of e-mail many of us receive. But three techniques really will make an immediate, dramatic, and sustainable change in how you review, process, and dispose of your e-mail.

> The goal is simple: empty your Inbox.
>
> Regularly.
>
> At least once a week.
>
> You can do it. Here's how.

Techniques For Getting "In To Empty"

I've studied many personal productivity methods over the years. The one system that has fundamentally changed the way I work is David Allen's *Getting Things Done*, or GTD as it's commonly labeled. GTD has become very popular with the tech and blogging communities in the past couple of years. Of the numerous reasons why David Allen's teachings are so popular with techies, road warriors, and knowledge workers, one jumps right out — we have a bigger e-mail problem than almost anyone else. Developing a way to consistently get our Inboxes empty is a critical skill we need to master.

We get more e-mail than most people. E-mail is an integral tool in our work. As a primary communications channel, e-mail is what we rely on to provide the essential raw material for our work—information. This information often requires action and, as I mentioned earlier, too many people are paralyzed into not processing and disposing of mail based on the fear that they won't be able to find something important at a later time.

So they leave everything in their Inbox! Does this sound familiar? If so, here are my questions for you if you regularly have more than ten or twenty e-mail messages in your Inbox:

1. Do you really think it's any easier to find what you're looking for in your Inbox?

2. If you have to scroll through screen after screen of mangled subject lines looking for something, are you really any better off than if you had dropped that message into another folder after reading it?

3. Have you really considered why you continue to do this?

Of course, my answer to these questions is no, no, and no. But let me expand on that third no. I think the principle reason people continue to use their Inbox as a big bucket is simply that it's what you first see when you launch your e-mail program. I'm horrified when I see someone's Inbox and it contains hundreds of unread messages and, in some cases, thousands of unfiled messages.

Thanks to some great ideas from David Allen and a number of other really bright people who have given this a lot of thought, I suggest three things you need to do to every piece of e-mail you receive—and leaving it in your Inbox is not one of them!

1. Read it.

2. Extract the action items it contains (if any).

3. File it.

If that sounds simple, it is. If that sounds overly simplistic . . . well, it is. Let me briefly expand on each step.

Read it: I don't mean read it as in "Your mission, should you decide to accept it, is to pore over every word, committing it to memory because this e-mail will self-destruct in fifteen seconds . . . good luck, Jim." What I mean is skim through the e-mail. If it's a reference e-mail like a newsletter, Web digest, commercial solicitation, or other nonessential communication, file it right away.

Create a folder called "Read & Review" in your e-mail client and put it in there. This only works if you exercise discipline and actually block out regular time out to read and review what you've placed in this folder. I do this twice a day—right after lunch and at the end of the day. It takes about fifteen minutes. If I'm having a really crazy week, I make sure to catch up on processing this folder during my Weekly Review (another key GTD idea) every Friday afternoon.

Important: Do not create new black holes by dumping e-mail into folders you never look at again. That is not processing, it's postponing. If you create a "Read & Review" folder, make a commitment to empty it at least once a week during your weekly review.

Extract tasks: If the e-mail contains an action you must take, create a new task immediately in Outlook or your PIM. This is one of the reasons I swear by Outlook. To create a new task, all I have to do is drag the e-mail message onto the Task icon. This creates a new task with all the information I might need related to that action. Right-click-and-drag provides an even richer set of options.

Edit the subject line of the task (it will initially be identical to the e-mail subject line) and use an action verb like reply or ship or call in the task description. Don't worry about formatting the task—that can be done as a separate activity. Just capture the action stuff and file the e-mail away. Review your task list as a separate activity every day and decide which items require a hard date and which can be done as time permits. I block out the first fifteen minutes of my day for this task review on my calendar—it's a standing appointment I make with myself.

File it: You can file it in a specific folder if that's the way you like to organize or you can simply drop it into a folder labeled "Read Mail." At one time I had a hierarchy in my Outlook message store that was five levels deep with more than two hundred folders. Trust me . . . you do not want to do this. Today, I have a folder hierarchy that is two levels deep and contains ten or twelve folders, depending on my current project load. Simpler is better.

I know . . . you're probably freaking out right about now, muttering to yourself something like "What is this guy—some kind of idiot? How will I ever find anything again if I just dump it into a folder like he suggests?" Don't freak out—I have a solution. Use a desktop search tool that indexes all your e-mail. Don't worry about filing everything in a carefully designed maze of folders. That virtually guarantees the one thing you're trying to avoid—losing stuff.

Think about how Google, Yahoo!, and other search engines have changed the way we use the Web. What is the first thing you do (online) when you need information? Why you "Google it," of course. Why not do the same thing on your PC? Up until very recently there was a good reason why most of us didn't trust search on our PCs—it didn't work!

The search tools built into Windows don't work for most people. It's not that they don't work at all, they are just difficult to use and return poor results unless you know a number of arcane tips and tricks. We now have tools that do a terrific job of indexing the information on our PCs. They look and work just like a Web search engine. A number of choices are available and almost all are free (visit www.astroprojects. com/morespace/marc for a list of these desktop search tools).

E-mail is an ideal file type for these search tools. E-mail messages are primarily text and are rich in keywords and metadata (attributes like sender, date sent, and so on). I can find any e-mail in a matter of seconds using my search tool.

You can find a wealth of information about working with information overload in the books I've listed in the "Recommended reading" list at the end of this chapter and online in blogs, discussion forums, and Web site articles. You can find many approaches to managing your Inbox, e-mail, and application files. Some use software. Some are technique-based. Picking the one that is right for you is a personal decision and some experimentation will probably be required before you find your best solution. What I've tried to provide here are some essential tips to get you started.

The "GTD Way"

I've mentioned *Getting Things Done* a number of times. In his book, David Allen describes a deceptively simple approach to productivity management and goal setting that I've been studying, practicing, and refining for four years. It has irrevocably changed the way I approach my work and my personal projects. It's outside my scope here to try to encapsulate the GTD system—and there's no need. Go pick up a copy of the book, visit the GTD Zone at OfficeZealot.com, or do an online search for "Getting Things Done" or "GTD" if you're interested in learning more.

For the purposes of this discussion about fixing e-mail, here's what I think is one of the most important lessons Allen teaches. It directly relates to the issue at hand—getting all the incoming stuff you have to deal with dealt with. Allen defines the following steps as his "Natural Planning Model." You can find an excellent workflow diagram of this process at his Web site, http://www.davidco.com. He has five steps:

1. Collect
2. Process
3. Organize
4. Review
5. Do

Allen concedes that these are things we probably do already. The important lesson he shares—and the one that I had failed to grasp (until a classic, forehead-slapping moment)—is that it is far more productive to focus on each step separately. Sometimes collecting stuff is the right thing to do; at other times, review is what's required.

Do one thing at a time, with focus, and avoid the temptation to mix these steps. For example, I find it all too easy to start "Do-ing" while I'm "Processing." I get a lot more accomplished when I stay on task and focus on processing when I'm in that mode and focus on doing when I'm ready to take action.

There's Nothing So Broken That It Can't Be Fixed

Fixing a broken, dysfunctional work environment may not be easy, but unlike many of the change initiatives you may have experienced (endured?), the payback for implementing some or all of these techniques is almost immediate, measurable, and self-sustaining. When I've shared some of these techniques through my blog or in consultation with other business people, the most common argument I get is that the person I'm talking with doesn't believe they have the power to make a meaningful change in their organization.

My response: "Nonsense—how will you know if you never try?" In *The Simplicity Survival Handbook*, Bill Jensen teaches a valuable lesson that ought to be obvious but often isn't. As he points out, happy, productive, low-stress people are a lot more fun to be around. People want to work with them, seek them out for their projects and teams, and look to them for advice and counsel. Why? Because deep inside, that's the state we all wish we could be in.

If you're at the bottom of the food chain and answerable to everyone but have authority over no one, focus on changing your own space. If you work in a team or manage a small group, implement these ideas on the small scale you do have control over. The positive environment you create in the space you can influence will be noticed. People will ask what you've been doing and why you (or your team or your department) always seems to be so much better prepared, productive, and pleasant to deal with.

I sometimes think about my old coworker Bill and wonder how he's faring in this new world of work. I'd like to think that he's learned a few things over the years and is now a better contributor to the teams he's involved with. I try to imagine his reaction were he to come to work at my company and the effect it would have on him. I like to think he'd see the value in working with an engaged team of people who have R-E-S-P-E-C-T for each other and a commitment to producing their best work with less stress and more fun.

I'll admit these topics have become something of an obsession for me. I write about them in my blogs, have gotten involved in developing curriculum to teach some of these principles to others, and am continually engaged in refining and reinventing more effective processes at my company. It's all too easy to tell yourself you can't change the way things are. But you can. Make an agreement with yourself that you will invest the time, energy, and discipline to make your life less stressful. How much would that be worth to you? To paraphrase the MasterCard commercial, my answer is "priceless."

Appendix - Contract For Communications

This is the introduction from the Contract for Communications we've developed at my company. The entire contract is rather lengthy (seven pages) and expands on the ideas expressed in this introduction. This excerpt will give you an idea of what such a document might address and codify for your organization.

Statement Of Purpose

We recognize that free and open communication is an essential ingredient for the continuing success of our company.

Communication can take many forms, from the chance meeting in the hallway where a question is asked and answered to the more formal scheduled meeting, and to open and vigorous debate of possible solutions to difficult problems. We strive to encourage all forms of communication. To make that communication more effective and to protect the dignity of individuals during vigorous debate, individuals are expected to follow the procedures and guidelines outlined here.

PROCEDURES

- Identify the purpose of the meeting.
- State the common goal at the beginning of the communication.
- Ensure that all persons have the ability to call a timeout at the beginning of the meeting.
- Ensure that all persons have the ability to call a two-minute timeout at any time.
- Agree to time constraints at the beginning of the communication.
- For more formal settings, designate a moderator, timekeeper, and note taker.
- During vigorous debate, summarize key points of continued disagreement at the midpoint of the meeting.
- Set reminders and reviews, if necessary, at the end of the communication.
- If multiple solutions were discussed, summarize and save the discarded solutions at the end of the meeting.

GUIDELINES

- The purpose of communication and debate is to generate a deeper understanding of key issues and produce a better end product or outcome.
- Ideas belong to the group, not the individual.
- Be respectful of others and their opinions and ideas.
- Do not interrupt the speaker.
- Do not hold a grudge.
- Ask questions instead of assuming.
- Be willing to play devil's advocate and understand that sometimes other people may also play this role.
- Being quiet is a sign that you are "okay." It is each person's responsibility to raise objections or state that he or she is still digesting the discussion material.
- Use inquiry to check on those less verbal in the group.
- Use a balanced approach when offering feedback ("Sandwich" negative points with positive points when critiquing).
- Be aware of the difference between feedback and unsolicited advice.
- Be honest, candid and forthcoming.
- Do not speak for others.
- Accept answers at face value and assume that people are working toward a common goal.
- Actively work on maintaining a win/win attitude during conflicts.

The contract also describes processes and procedures for using e-mail effectively, scheduling and conducting meetings, making effective use of voice mail and more.

For a complete copy of the contract visit www.astroprojects.com/morespace/marc.

FROM THE EDITOR

I held a contest for one slot in this book. Marc holds the honor of filling that spot. I wasn't familiar with his work before the contest, but just try a Google search of "Marc Orchant" and see how many thousand results you get. You will find him writing about Microsoft Office, Tablet PCs, and his friend and mentor David Allen. His title at the software company where he works is "Chief Storyteller" (I have always loved that). He has lived by Carlsbad Caverns (New Mexico) for a quarter of a century!

In His Own Words . . .

What is it about your essay topic that made you want to write this chapter in *More Space*?

"I have the great fortune to work for a most unusual company—a company populated by some of the smartest and most passionate people I've ever worked with. Together, we have addressed many of the things that are broken for so many people in their workplace and created sustainable solutions that have proven to be portable and reproducible. My *More Space* essay is an attempt to codify some of these ideas and practices in a format that can be shared with a wide range of organizations. I firmly believe that work doesn't have to take place in a toxic environment and that it is possible to create a workplace that provides challenges and opportunities for professional and personal growth in any organization, regardless of size or niche. I hope to use my *More Space* essay as the centerpiece of a proposal for *Work Is Broken,* the book I'm planning to write next."

Marc's blog:
blogs.officezealot.com/marc

Marc's favorite blogs:
www.Buzzmachine.com
sethgodin.typepad.com
www.davidco.com/blogs/david/

Recommended reading:

Getting Things Done
by David Allen

Ready for Anything
by David Allen

Beyond Bullet Points
by Cliff Atkinson

How to Mind Map: Make the Most of Your Mind and Learn to Create, Organize and Plan
by Tony Buzan

Six Thinking Hats
by Edward De Bono

More Balls Than Hands
by Michael Gelb

Survival Is Not Enough: Zooming, Evolution, and the Future of Your Company
by Seth Godin

The Simplicity Survival Handbook
by Bill Jensen

Re-imagine!
by Tom Peters

The Inevitability Of Authenticity

by Jory Des Jardins

It was 2002 in San Francisco, meaning everyone who used to work south of Market Street was now unemployed. At the time I was in between jobs and would prattle on endlessly to my friend Calvin about how poor I was. Calvin is a soft, technologically oriented man in his fifties; we'd met at a personal development workshop a year before and often got together for lunch in the City, or on the Peninsula where he worked, to talk about relationships and writing.

He saw me eyeing one of his cell phones.

"You want it?" he said. "I got it on eBay." I suspected Calvin spent more time buying used electronics than he did working.

"No, no, of course not," I said, embarrassed. "I was just looking."

Calvin always listened attentively, providing me with inspiring books to read during my imposed sabbatical, and offered his own form of unemployment insurance—a subsidized lunch check. When the bill arrived at the end of every shared meal he'd say, "Put down your co-pay," and I'd hand him five bucks.

Today he broke the monotony and told me about a job opening at his company. I was surprised by his candidness; he'd spent fifteen years at the company but had not one whit of promotional rah rah to offer.

"I'm not promising you a new career," he said. "The company is in trouble. I'm not even sure I like where it's going. I can only promise you an income." It was enough.

"Do you need my résumé?" I asked, unsure of what Calvin could possibly tell the hiring manager about me other than I had a tortured past with men and was desperate for a job.

"Shoot me a résumé for HR's purposes," he said. "But I've already told them about you. We could really use someone with your communication skills."

Skills? What skills? As far as I was concerned, skills came from trying. Skills were about tangible things—closing sales, completing projects on time and on budget. I'd only gone into job interviews with facts and figures. I was nervous; what would I bring? Pay stubs from the unemployment office to prove just how needy I was?

My first interview went poorly. I was told the position required an element of selling, but mostly customer relationship skills. I flew to LA to meet with the head of sales, which frightened me a bit—I was hoping to chat with someone on the cost center versus the revenue-generating side of the business, as I relate to those folks better. People in sales always struck me as a bit heartless, disembodied from the product. I'd worked in publishing for years but spent most of my career on the fulfillment end of the contract; getting the business was someone else's problem. I reassured myself with what Calvin had told me over lunch; the company was rethinking its approach to fit a more solution-oriented sales strategy, as opposed to its previous "take it or leave it" attitude. The company was notorious for producing the priciest events in the tech industry. During the dot-com boom they could get away with it—you'd be a fool not to hawk your product next to Apple's booth in front of twenty-five thousand qualified leads, even if you had to sell your youngest child to do it.

"I've told them forever that our arrogance couldn't last," Calvin said to me. "We heard the grumblings when things were good, but no one listens when you're making money hand over fist."

Now, however, the company was in bankruptcy proceedings. Its former shoo-in customers, the top tech companies, were finding that smaller, more intimate and customized events were yielding better results—for less money—than the Cirque du Soleil-like extravaganzas that Calvin's company produced. The smaller clients had other things to think about, like making payroll. Calvin's company had made so many acquisitions during the years of irrational exuberance that it simply couldn't afford them any longer.

Still, bankruptcy was a step up from unemployment.

"They still have health insurance, right?" I asked Calvin. As long as my paycheck cleared, I couldn't care less about the company's history. I took Calvin's warnings with a grain of salt.

Calvin explained that they wanted someone who could close deals, yes, but who would also stick with a handful of their largest clients and continually monitor and grow the relationships. I imagined myself kvetching with product managers and faxing them contracts.

"You're right, Calvin," I said. "I am perfect for this job."

I received a call later that day from an HR person who wanted to schedule an interview.

"Can you make it to our Los Angeles office?" she said.

"Sure. What day?"

"Tomorrow. At 8:30 A.M."

I looked at my watch—it was 4:30 in the afternoon. Wow, I thought, they mean business.

That night I hardly slept, I was so anxious, but I finally succumbed to my insomnia and got out of bed at 3:30 A.M. to make the 6 A.M. flight. Needless to say, by 8:30 A.M. I was a bit out of it, and the gallon of Starbucks I'd chugged at the airport was acting more like a diuretic than a stimulant.

I arrived at the interview decidedly underdressed. Calvin always wore Dockers and a button-down shirt to work, so I wore an uncontroversial plain cardigan sweater over black slacks. I had been told the head of sales "could fit in twenty or thirty minutes." I tried to bullet-point my skills in my head during the flight so that I would be as concise as possible. While I waited in the glass-walled lobby I recited them in my head.

The VP's assistant came out to greet me in a suit. He smelled of expensive cologne.

"He's ready to see you now, Jory," he said.

My first thought was, "Shit."

I met Jerry, the vice president of sales, with a firm but clammy handshake.

I don't remember much of what happened, only that my bullet points were irrelevant. All that highfalutin name-dropping I had intended for the first five minutes was pushed to the wayside by his immediate questions.

"So, Jory, the San Francisco office speaks very highly of you; though I must admit some concern. I don't see any sales experience on your résumé."

"Oh I've had plenty. At my last company we all had to pitch in and cold call. However, my experience has been much more in working with the client. I've developed programs for quite a few companies and grown those relationships."

"But did you close sales?"

"Not per se, no. I grew them."

"That's not closing the sale."

"No, I suppose not."

"Let me be blunt, Jory. We need a closer. Someone who has closed at least $3 million in annual sales and who has considerable cold calling experience—at least eighteen months. I don't see that here. I'm still trying to make sense of what you have down here near the bottom of your résumé."

In an attempt to completely alter my past for this interview I shoved my previous seven years of magazine editing and writing experience into a few lines, even shrinking the font. I wanted to tell him that, having sold advertising in an all-hands sales effort during my last job, a dot-com in its final tailspin, I had developed the skill of bullshitting my way through anything. And while $3 million worth of bullshit was certainly a lot of bullshit, it wasn't insurmountable. In fact, I could probably make the company that much thinking of ways to save money. Let's start with a ban on dragging people on airplanes for twenty-minute meetings. . . .

But I didn't say anything. I just nodded empathetically, hoping he would take exception to my lacking background because of my ability to take it like a man, not a sniveling, soft-skilled woman.

I was back on a plane by 10 A.M. and back in San Francisco by noon. No sooner had I entered my apartment when I received a call on my cell phone from Calvin.

"How'd it go?" he said.

"Don't ask."

"Yeah, I thought I'd hear it from you first. . . . I got the feedback from Jerry's office."

"Thrill."

"I have good news and bad news."

"You know me—start with the bad."

"Jerry didn't like you."

"Geeze. . . . What's the good news?"

"We don't like Jerry."

I got the job.

It seemed so strange to me that I had "won" the majority of folks over without so much as telling a white lie to spiff up my qualifications. I was taken "as is," like one of the many flawed electronic gadgets Calvin bought on eBay.

It occurred to me that what I perceived to be my flaws—in this case my vulnerability around Calvin—was my strength. Calvin didn't help get me a job because I was "a closer" but because he knew me and could relate to me—so much so that he convinced others at the company that I was a worthy investment. All the struggles I'd shared with him further cemented in his mind my ability to connect with customers. He'd known all along that I would crash and burn in that interview; it was my utter incompatibility with Mr. $3 Million that sealed the deal.

★ ★ ★ ★

Like I said earlier, I'd met Calvin at a personal development workshop. We'd gone for different reasons. He'd gone because he'd had a near-fatal heart attack just a few months before. Obviously, he'd survived, but things were different. He knew that his condition had, in part, been a result of the stress he'd placed on himself to perform. Not to do work as such but literally to perform, to be someone he wasn't. He wanted more clarity on just who Calvin really was.

I went for business reasons; the company that produced the seminar was a potential client, and they invited me to attend, gratis, to better understand their "product." My boss at the time had thought that attending would be good for growing the business relationship, so they sent me—on Memorial Day weekend, no less—to represent our firm. I sat through the first few hours very pissed off. I read self-help books all the time and knew this routine cold. It would only be a matter of time before they'd ask me to start punching something.

I sat next to a red-haired woman who, I could smell, was dying for a smoke. The first moment of freedom we both beelined to the front door and stood in the unappreciated sunshine.

"Is this a lot of crap or what?" she said, lighting up.

"I wonder if they'll notice if I sneak out," I said.

"Yeah. My husband made me go to this; I don't know why. I suppose he thinks it will make me a better listener or something. Why'd you come?"

"Strictly business, I assure you."

"What do you mean? You work for the company?"

"Me? No. They're a client . . . potential client. We might do an advertising campaign for them. Supposedly this will help me better understand them." Somehow, by introducing myself as someone who would never be so desperate as to actually pay for one of these seminars I was washing myself of that human funk I smelled on the others. After all, I had been told my whole life that I had my shit together. And now I had a well-paying, director-level job to prove it. I'd been a magazine writer, but after slogging it out for little pay and being rejected by clueless people for a while, it became very clear to me I needed to aspire elsewhere. The company I was working for, which would become a blip in the dot-com cosmos just a few short months later, had made for a great ego shelter the past few years.

Despite my threats to leave I stayed. What would I possibly say to my boss if I abandoned our mission of good will? That I was above this crap? She was accustomed to jumping on planes at the beck and call of clients. All I needed to do was keep my butt in a chair.

Throughout the day, I writhed and repositioned myself in my unforgiving stackable chair. A few of the workshop participants had brought cushions; I wondered if any of them would be willing to sell me theirs. Food was not allowed in the room, but I crammed bits of protein bar into my mouth whenever the course leader looked away. After a few hours, however, as more people shared themselves with the group, I forgot about my discomfort; I became interested in their stories, even a bit impressed. There were a few CEOs, entrepreneurs who'd just sold their companies and, now very wealthy and with their lives wide open to possibility, struggled to find the next, meaningful step; a few very young people with woo-woo parents who wanted their kids to get a dose of this self-awareness stuff early, preferably before they were my age.

The next break I ate lunch with folks who were more up than my last break mate. One was an executive coach who said he was reviewing the course. He'd taken it before three years earlier.

"Which part did you forget?" I asked him, "the incessant repetition or sitting for fifteen hours in uncomfortable chairs?" He just smiled, and maybe laughed at me.

I noticed the red-haired woman I had been sitting next to was nowhere to be seen. Shame, she seemed to actually need this shit. As annoyed as I was by being here, I was finding my social tendencies kicking in; I was actually enjoying my conversations with people. And some of the content was interesting, much the way it's interesting to sit in on a focus group, to examine the state of others. I always thought of myself as somewhat of a pulse taker. Someone who could observe, synthesize, and then create something that "spoke" for the people I'd observed. I did that a lot as a magazine writer, often writing articles on stuff I'd read about that seemed to be compelling to somebody; unfortunately, the content bored me. Sometimes I wondered if it bored my readers as a result. And, well, I'd rather be dead than boring.

I sat with another woman, a nice girl for sure, but a bit weepy. She kept a box of Kleenex under her chair, which was nearly used up, and we were only on Day One. By the end of the first grueling day the instructors told us that we'd be all over the map in terms of our emotional levels. Some of us would be racing at the top of the roller coaster; others would be low, or maybe even confused. I thought: Smart tactic to get people to come back—make them think that it's all part of the "process."

We were asked to call a family member that night and share an "inauthenticity." I'm usually very good with homework assignments, but I was confused. I didn't think I had any reason to call someone. I dialed my twin sister from my bed. She lives in Boston, three hours ahead, and seemed annoyed.

"Hello," she said, barely awake.

"It's me."

"It's late."

"I know. I know. Just humor me . . . So I'm taking that workshop this weekend, and I'm supposed to call someone and share something inauthentic about myself. . . . Do you think I have anything to share?"

"I don't know. You seem to tell people things whether they want to hear them or not."

"I know! I'm a fairly straight shooter, right?"

"Maybe you can call someone who knew your ex?" My stomach dropped when I heard that.

"Why would I do that? What else is there to discuss about that? It's over. Done."

"All right. You just asked if there was something you could share. It seemed like that could be something."

"This homework assignment is stupid."

"Yeah, no shit. It's two in the morning here."

"OK. So, for the record I called you, we determined that there was nothing for me to share, no inauthenticities, and we're cool."

"Fine. Good night."

The second day I wore something a bit more casual. I had an odd feeling that I'd need to wear clothes that weren't so binding; something that I wouldn't mind crying in. The executive coach had warned me that the second day can get very emotional for people. I figured, I cry at movies, and with all this raw, frightening emotion I was likely to witness today you just never know.

The course instructors seemed to be getting mighty personal with the morons who opted to get up and share with the rest of the crowd. As expected, some broke into tears. I could smell my sweat when this occurred. I just listened and applauded on cue, at the end of each gripping bit of testimony.

We had some sort of visualization exercise that I cannot share, not only to maintain the privacy of the people I met in the seminar, but because I truly don't remember it. All I remember was the hit, directly in my stomach and rising. We had to keep our eyes closed, as I suppose the point was to have an experience untainted by worries of being watched. Still, I felt a pang of embarrassment, even shame. I became aware, beyond any way that my brain could comprehend, in my body, of the absurdity of my life.

A beautiful story rolled out in front of me—so good I'd wished I'd written it instead of lived it—of a girl so plastic you could knock on her, and very pretty. She made sure of it. She lived a plastic life and wondered why she couldn't feel very much. People liked to be around her, but only for so long—shit, she was plastic! How long can it hold your interest, really?

Our eyes were still closed. My cheeks were wet; I must have started crying. And I felt a weight, literally, coming from my nose. I shook my head and felt a soft, wet pull. I broke ranks and opened my eyes. The room was full of people with closed eyes, some crying, and a pendulous, two-foot-long globule of snot was hanging from my right nostril. The others couldn't see it, but the seminar leaders couldn't have missed it. How unattractive! The Plastic Girl has snot coming out of her nose! The Plastic Girl is absurd. Boy that was funny. So funny I felt a chuckle coming on and then a full-out belly laugh. A few of the others started joining me.

We were asked if we wanted to share our experience. I didn't, I thought, and yet I walked to the microphone at the front of the room. I felt I owed these people an explanation. I looked up; a room full of people were looking at me. Their eyes hurt, but I let them take me in, snot and all. I hadn't rehearsed anything in my head. What the hell would I possibly say? Even I was surprised by what came out, the sound of my voice.

"I'm a good writer," I said. "But I'll never get it down on paper. Ever." I decided to tell these people the story of the Plastic Girl. Several months before the seminar she had been dating a coworker who could best be described as different from her. He wasn't your average professional. His hair was longer than hers. He was wicked smart and wicked rude. She liked the fact that he was rude. Some people at the company called him an asshole, which they felt perfectly comfortable calling him around her, as they assumed she had no connection to him whatsoever. They never spoke to each other in the office, never saw each other in the vicinity of the office. They kept the personal and the professional completely separate, walled off with Fort Knox–like security.

One day he gives the Plastic Girl some very bad news that he has just discovered; he is HIV positive. The information bounces off of her, as there is no place for it to be taken in. Surely, she being Plastic, she cannot contract such horrific things as HIV. She reacts by pretending he doesn't have a virus and hoping that he will learn to do the same, or accept his condition and stop being so emotional all the time. Weeks later his body was found in the park, hanging from a tree. The sound of plastic cracking was deafening.

The funeral, the HIV testing, and the therapy sessions that followed chipped away at her some more. Since his death she just hadn't been feeling like her usual plasticky self. She felt soft and mushy. Her usual unquestioned get-up-and-go was more tenuous.

I told them my overriding concern at my boyfriend's funeral was whether my mascara was waterproof. I told them that the greatest compliment you could give me in the last few months is, "Despite it all, she looks great."

I sat down and the Weepy Woman hugged me. I didn't feel I deserved to be hugged. I felt sick to my stomach, and ugly. I could feel my face had puffed up from the tears.

At the break people kept coming up to me. One man said he didn't know why but he just wanted to hug me. The executive coach asked me out.

A tall, scruffy man approached me, "Wow, that was some story. It's a shame you stopped writing. If you decide to start up again I'd love to help." He extended his hand, "My name is Calvin."

I returned to work that Tuesday.

"How was the seminar?" my boss asked me. "I hope it didn't completely blow your weekend."

"It was fine. Real nice."

"No one made you drink the purple Kool-Aid, did they?"

"Nope. It was cherry."

"Hah. That's the spirit. Brief us later in the staff meeting."

"Yeah, sure."

I thought about what I would say. Frankly I had no new insights as to how we would win over the client. I suppose they'd won me over. I understood why they invited me to their seminar. How can you work for clients whose language you do not share? I'd thought I knew their language, but until this weekend I had been speaking in tongues. I wasn't speaking Human.

★   ★   ★   ★

A couple of months after I took the job at Calvin's company, I noticed he'd maintained this cheapo Web site called a Web log that he posted copy to every day.

"What is it?" I asked him, "Are you selling products?"

"No. I just like to post my opinions."

I thought he was naive. What if someone lifted his stuff and posted it to their site? Would he get royalties? I told him he should keep his best stuff for print.

"These aren't articles I'm posting. These are conversations," he said. "You can't wait to get these in print. They happen in real time."

Anything to avoid work, I thought. Calvin posted to his blog constantly, typically in the middle of meetings, from his laptop or BlackBerry, any way he could. He often sent me links to stories or commentary. I always sent him brief thank-you notes for sending them, but I never read the stuff. I used my spare time reading trade Web sites that focused on tech trends the company covered for the industry. From these sites I learned who mattered, and who I needed to pursue.

Everyone knew Calvin had checked out of the quotidian aspects of his job a long time ago. From a manager's standpoint the only reason he woke up every morning was to surf on eBay for bargains or post to "his little Web site." The first time that I visited Calvin's office I was shocked at all of the bells and whistles he liked to use, or to just collect. There must have been three BlackBerrys on his desk, four cell phones, two servers (one for his personal use, he later explained), two desktops, and a laptop. Despite all of his gadgets, he never used them to record deadlines, to-do lists, and project plans. At times I was quite irritated with Calvin; when he failed to show up at meetings people would come to my desk looking for him.

Once he missed a meeting that I had scheduled with one of our most promising clients.

I don't usually confront senior executives, but Calvin was so clueless (or approachable—I hadn't yet made the distinction) that I confronted him about his flakiness.

"I told them you would be in that meeting," I said to him. "How are we going to get to their decision makers if we can't even convince the gatekeepers?"

"Sorry," Calvin said. "Who do you want to reach at that company?" I told him.

"Tell you what," he said. "Let me call him. We're friends."

The bottom line was, despite his flakiness, Calvin was a hot commodity, the guy you would go to when you wanted to score a meeting with some pooh-bah at Apple or Adobe. These muckety-mucks blew off us sales types, but when Calvin called they cut out of meetings, or if they couldn't talk at that moment, they always called back.

I often had to broker sales through Calvin, even though he wasn't in sales, because the contact refused to talk to anyone but him. I would often write notes to him during teleconferences with potential customers, listing instructions to help move along the conversations. He never followed my instructions, but he did close deals. It didn't matter what Calvin was requesting of them; it seemed that as long as the words came from him, they were gold. Once, when I'd asked Calvin to accompany me to an off-site pitch meeting, our general manager quipped, half-joking, "Make sure he's wearing a clean shirt." Still, there was no question that Calvin should attend.

There was something powerful about this man who eschewed appearances. Calvin had a secret "in", and no one thought to question where it came from. He seemed to know more than where a person worked or his position in a company. He knew them personally, and he knew the real stories behind their trade-publication announcements. He knew that some VP I wanted to get a meeting with had a long-standing grudge against our company for an article we produced touting a competitor's new product release.

"How did you know this?" I asked Calvin, thinking he'd read this in some insider column available for an exorbitant subscription fee.

"He told me," Calvin said.

Calvin also knew who was disappointed with the events we held for the industry, which speakers tanked, what the word on the street was about our new launching event in Amsterdam. Yet he never polled, surveyed, or hired a marketing team to find out our customers' perception of us, nor did he ask. They simply told him. And in return he told them things that he knew about hot products, open jobs, must-see demos. Despite all that he was told, it seemed the debt of information owed him was always greater. Not like he was keeping track; I was.

I wondered why Calvin hadn't helped us to leverage these contacts sooner. I also questioned his sanity: What the hell are contacts for if not to drum up business?

★　　★　　★　　★

I went to a follow-up to the seminar where I met Calvin, as I felt like something inside me had cracked open that Memorial Day Weekend, and this unintelligible crap was oozing out—old memories and strange, entrepreneurial desires. I was seeing something but couldn't yet make it out.

The next seminar I attended was not quite as visceral as the first. Most of the people there were ready to explore themselves and less resistant to being there. Many of the sessions were interesting discourses, almost like college lectures. One discussion that interested me, in particular, was about authenticity; more specifically about being authentic.

This discussion made me nervous. I had suspected I had authenticity issues, but what does it mean to be *inauthentic*? I'd always tried to beat people in quantifiable ways: get more money, get more promotions, or get better evaluations. But, on occasion, I found myself in situations where people were simply not impressed. And nothing I could say or do could change it. I usually referred to these people as weird, or naive. Something just wasn't right about them.

I had been warned by another attendee about the course leader. "She'll kick your ass," he said. I wondered what he meant. She was tall and slim. Granted, I'm short, but I fight nasty. Physically I could take her.

Over the course of the day I started to understand. The woman wasn't so much an ass-kicker as a bullshit detector. People shared some mighty strong insights and stories about themselves. I'd come out as a crier and now had my box of tissues planted under my chair. Wads of wet Kleenex were starting to pile up underneath. But with some of the most convincing people she would stand and look at them with her arms crossed and her nose wrinkled, like she'd smelled something bad.

"Nope," she'd say. "I don't buy it."

I spent that first day with my mouth agape. Here people were opening themselves up to inquiry, sharing themselves, and getting shot down like plastic ducks in a carnival game. It seemed irresponsible to me, her behavior. Once again, I feared sharing myself. What if everything I'd believed about myself and shared in an effort to show my vulnerability was rejected, labeled inauthentic? Oh, the horror.

A new word was used at the seminar and regarded as the worst insult you could place on someone: "Sincere." It held a new meaning in this seminar, not the dictionary meaning. In this room, *sincere* meant its very opposite, or a bland attempt at authenticity. If someone shared something and was told they were very sincere they immediately dropped their shoulders in defeat. While I was hardly an expert, I started to see a pattern in everyone who was dubbed sincere. Usually they had devised some story about themselves about why they were so alone, or fat, or unhappy, and it was usually very *very* sad. When they spoke I thought of *Beaches* and other movies that made me cry, of the music that often played in the background. It played behind these people while they spoke.

On the flip side, some of the people I thought had not one whit of charisma got away scot-free. If they were asked a question, they might have said, "I don't know," or given a very plain vanilla answer. They had so little sense of story about them; they didn't see themselves as ingenues or characters in a melodrama that were put upon by the world. The reaction the leader had with them was always the same, "Thanks very much for sharing." My reaction was always, Booooooooorrrrring!

My goal for the day was twofold—to be able to come to this mind-blowing epiphany about myself and then to have the course leader smile at me and say, "Thanks very much for sharing." The question was, how? I couldn't quite make out what it took to be authentic, the secret sauce.

"Jory!" Her voice was so loud, I thought. I looked at her like a deer in headlights.

"You've been quiet today. Why don't you come up here and share your thoughts on authenticity with the group?"

I walked up to the microphone, concerned about my underwear. I'd worn a pair that

This discussion made me nervous. I had suspected I had authenticity issues, but what does it mean to be *inauthentic*?

tended to creep up. My voice sounded shaky, scared.

"Yes?" I said into the microphone.

"Yes what? I have no questions for you. I just thought it would be nice to hear your thoughts on the discussion."

"About authenticity?"

"Sure."

"Well . . . I just realize that I have been living my life as a very sincere person. I haven't been very real. I say what I think other people want to hear."

"Really?"

"Yes."

"Thank you for sharing, Jory. Your comments were very *sincere*."

"Scuse me?"

"You heard me. . . . Tell me, did I catch you at a bad time?"

"I'm not sure I follow."

"It seems I didn't allow you enough time to rehearse."

Shit. This wasn't happening.

"I'm not sure what to say," I said.

"I can see that."

"OK, so it's like a damned-if-you-do, damned-if-you-don't thing, is that it? I'm being totally straight with you, but if I say anything, it's not authentic, it's sincere."

"Not necessarily; just what you are saying now."

"Fine then, I just won't say anything."

(Silence.)

The leader said, "Now you are being sincerely indignant."

"What the fuck do you want from me?! Not to speak? Not to be silent? I don't know what you want, OK? I don't know what you want!"

"Now you sound angry. *Sincerely* angry."

I put my head down and pouted to myself. The silence wasn't maddening, however. I didn't feel like I was wasting people's time. The moments felt necessary.

"I'm so frustrated," I said, surprised by the weakness of my own voice. "I want to say the right thing, but I can't. I'm not sure I know how to be authentic. I'm worried that I never will be real. I've been this way for so long. Practiced."

The course leader smiled, "Thanks very much for sharing, Jory. You can have your seat now."

They hired a new guy to be my direct supervisor at the company. I had been working at the firm now for two months with hardly any supervision. I'm a fairly independent worker and used the time well to bone up on the industry, but I was ready to delve into working with clients. I had been told not to make any calls yet, as the general manager was still working out significant changes in the product. Revolutionary changes, actually.

I'd listened in on his meetings with our largest clients and was quite impressed: He seemed to be the epitome of what I had promised to be this job around, a good listener. We'd been arrogant, he said. We were ready to get real with our customers and give them what they wanted. We'd been receiving their feedback now for months, and soon we would unveil our new product, a conference that drew only the most qualified leads and that didn't require a huge investment. At the end of every call, I thought to myself, "Shit, sounds great, but how?"

I was impressed with our humility and insistence on creating a "customer experience"; when potential clients called to ask about the upcoming show, I toed the company line. "We've been taking in all of your feedback and incorporating it into plans for the new show," I said. "We're still working out the details, so I can't share much with you now. But the changes are going to be big. Real big."

Our largest client was in my territory. I did all the groundwork to reestablish contact with the client, set up phone calls, and connect with the primary decision maker. It almost seemed too easy, when I got a simple, one-line e-mail from a marketing manager who wrote, "Can you talk at 1p today?"

I forwarded the note to my boss, who would hopefully have something to say, as I had no clue yet what our product was. We figured this woman was a gatekeeper—by the sound of her title she clearly was—and we just needed to keep her on the hook long enough to get to her boss. By then we'd have a better idea of the value proposition and would probably have pulled together some glossy materials.

The meeting was fairly brief. She asked very basic questions about the product. My boss was good—he practically crafted the package as he spoke, throwing in special features that would "increase their traction" at the event. She was a dutiful peon, asking if we had any figures that backed up what he was saying.

"How can I?" my boss said. "No one is doing this yet. However, I understand your concerns. Normally this would be a $500K package. But we're realistic about things these days. We know we're asking our clients to take a huge leap. We also know that gone are the days of the million-dollar trade show booths. I'll have Jory put together a proposal, but it's probably going to be a $250K package."

Wow, I thought, what a value.

"That won't be necessary," she said. "I'll just need a term sheet. You can fax me the contract." Apparently, this "gatekeeper" had the keys to the safe deposit box as well. She made this whole sales thing look easy. She faxed the contract back, signed. Just a few more of these, I thought, and I've blown away my quota. This sale, I felt, was proof that our insistence on being real with customers, on letting them know that we'd heard them, was going to help us blow our numbers out of the water.

In reality, we'd just sold a bill of goods to our largest client, and now we had to bullshit from there. The products that sold from that point on were not actually built as a response to client feedback; they were hybrids of the product we'd just sold our largest client. Unfortunately, these products didn't match what the other companies needed. Some companies that directly competed with this company were pissed that they hadn't been given first dibs, or any say in the matter. I told them all the same thing, the same thing I'd heard my boss say:

"We've incorporated your feedback over the past few months and the product reflects your concerns."

"What concerns?" said one particularly argumentative customer. "I never asked for this! A turnkey solution? I never asked you to save me money at the expense of displaying my brand!"

It was a particularly painful meeting. My boss and I had actually flown to see this client with the expectation of closing them, as the company had every year for the past five years. "They need us," is how it was explained to me, when I first brought up the concerns they had not-subtly relayed to me via e-mail, when I introduced our revolutionary turnkey product.

We left the gilded lobby of the company smiling—at least until we got to the parking lot.

"God," my boss said. "They are so trade show. We need to get over their heads and start talking to folks who actually understand this shit."

Unfortunately for us, those *were* the decision makers; the "grunts" that we spoke to every day, who stood on the trade show floors for hours on end. Their management gave purchasing authority for that very reason—they lived the product. Still, we were convinced that we just needed to rationalize with someone with a director or higher title, someone who understood what was happening in the market. Someone who wouldn't react like a child to change.

Meanwhile, Calvin tapped away on his blog and, on occasion, provided insight into what some of our larger clients were thinking. We'd learned that another big client of ours highly distrusted our management and was blowing off our calls.

"I think they want us to prove this new concept of ours before taking it on like a guinea pig," he told me. "Maybe we should let them pass this time around, or maybe we should just let them have it for next to nothing until we do right in their eyes again."

"Oh, that would go over well, Calvin," I said. "We've got $2.4 million to clear this year. How are we going to get there if we let one of our biggest clients get the product for free?"

"Those numbers are apparitions from a time we're no longer living in," Calvin said. Ultimately, he kept these opinions to himself. He wasn't exactly the Norma Rae of the office, more like the creeping wise man. You had to visit him in his cluttered lair and be willing to put up with rants against George Bush before getting an ounce of customer insight.

I can't say I blamed him. People in the office tended to shut down when they heard threatening information. If it came from a customer we sent them a bottle of wine before shutting down. If it came from an employee that person was treated like a leper. I'd seen a few people leave in ignominy, for what I'm not sure.

Tension was rising in the office, and now my boss's boss was wondering why we weren't making our numbers. We had, after all, scored an early win and pulled in a big client. We'd listened to customers and had eaten humble pie. Why couldn't we pull in the rest of the usual players? Clearly, the sales team wasn't doing their job.

One morning there was a lined sheet of notebook paper taped to my boss's office door. It was a sign-up sheet. We had to sign out and back in any time we took a break, including bathroom breaks that took longer than ten minutes.

"Guess that rules out taking a decent shit," said one of my colleagues.

I was starting to feel the pinch, or more accurately, the quick rush of air before the axe fell. When the "we've listened to your feedback" line failed to go over, we resorted to quick-and-dirty appeasement. Several of the big players I had brought in were now complaining about their deals. They'd heard that we'd offered a competitor ten feet more space to close a deal, and another company the ability to hang their sign when the rest weren't allowed to brand their booths. Some threatened to pull out of the show.

"I could have told you all this would happen," Calvin told me, over lunch. "They all speak to each other."

"But they are all competitors! Why would they do that?"

Calvin laughed at me. I was starting to understand. On purely a commodity level, every company is the same, and they only have their personal legacies to differentiate themselves. By providing a turnkey solution that allowed none of the companies to compete, we'd made sure they had no other leverage but to turn to each other and cooperate.

And there was something else, something even stronger than business theory. We had banked on a few assumptions, namely that companies will do anything to compete. They'd pay more money to look better than their competitors, and they'd keep their mouths shut about it. What we hadn't banked on was the human factor: the fact that these "Trade Show Folks" went to the same events—ten, twenty, thirty a year. They stayed at the same hotels and had beers with each other after long days on the floor. They talked about their kids and the goddamned drayage and union costs they were charged to set up their booths. They sniffed out the bullshitters. We'd never really asked them what they wanted; we just assumed we knew. And then we sold them something that showed we'd never really bothered to ask. We'd been very, very *sincere*.

The show was a week away.

"It's going to be a long week," I said.

The first day of the conference conjures up for me visions of the American Revolution. I'd seen movies like *Glory* and *The Patriot* and was always bewildered by how the British practically walked to their deaths wearing garish red uniforms, knowingly marching into excruciating pain. I stood there with my colleagues, taking a deep breath, about to march—'scuse me—walk the show floor and greet our clients. We wore stiff pantsuits and, as my boss required, hard-soled shoes. They were the Americans, wearing casual, logoed Polo shirts and comfortable shoes. I wanted to linger in the back and let the other sales folks take the first shots.

One of the people in operations ran over like a loyal decoy.

"I just finished helping your client set up. Shit, Jory, she . . . is . . . pissed. I told her you'd be right over to chat with her."

Another operations person, who had been working with another of my clients, took me aside with more diplomacy, "I think I quelled them for now, but they are definitely going to want to vent about a few things. I think they have a list," she said.

I relayed this information to my boss, asking for his input on how we should handle this rare, direct contact with the client. They were no longer pains-in-the-ass whose phone calls we could ignore until we thought up some special amenity we could throw into their contract.

"No worries," he said, though I knew him better now and could tell this was just a reaction. "Set up a meeting."

It got worse. The grumblings miraculously trickled upward, to my boss's boss. I was asked to "make room for a few more chairs" at our feedback meeting.

I saw Calvin, who had been busy with the content side of the conference, and told him about my date with death at approximately 1 P.M. He giggled like a schoolboy. I knew that he wished me no ill will; it was only that his suspicions had been validated. Although the show he'd spent years developing was quickly crumbling at his feet, he felt a strange satisfaction in having had the clairvoyance to see it happening months, maybe even years, before.

The meetings we held with these important clients were anything but fun, as having your maw stuffed with humble pie is often rather painful. I did what any smart person would do and kept my mouth shut and took notes. My boss offered an ounce of resistance by making some claim that he hadn't said what had been attributed to him by the client; unfortunately the Lilliputians had taken plenty of notes during our initial pitch to them and had documented the conversations.

At the end my boss's boss, a smart lady who had also kept her mouth shut during the proceedings, asked if I had written down all the customer complaints.

"Yes," I said. "All seventy—I'm sorry, seventy-one—points." The only thing I had said the whole meeting, and I don't think it was appreciated.

One of the clients—one we'd determined was too low level to take seriously, had spoken the entire time. She had been in her position with the company for twenty-five years. Long enough, I suppose, to have seen it all. Longer than me, my boss, and his boss combined.

"Do you get that we have been on board with your company for years, through thick and through thin?" she said, looking more hurt than angry. "We want you to be successful; your events have done that for us in the past. Do you know what it feels like to be lied to all of the time?"

Needless to say our GM was humbled by all of this; he said, "We plan to make up for all of this. We are currently planning a summit for our best customers. We'll fly them to a resort, on our dime, of course, and try to figure out where we went wrong. And we intend to collect every ounce of feedback and incorporate it into our next event."

I thought to myself: Wow, why wasn't I told about this summit. But then I remembered how we got into this whole mess in the first place: by pretending we'd listened. This was just the same old line, different day.

The war ended, as most do, with a lot of carnage—in this case amid the rubble of dismantled trade show booths. Numerous key personnel were asked to leave shortly afterward, including Calvin. I was not fortunate enough to get fired, so I left of my own volition, surprised that I had managed to find a job to replace this one. When I started to refashion my résumé I didn't know what to say, what was my title? Strategic Account Manager? Propagandist?

My last day at the company I snuck out early, had a drink with a friend, went home, and took a very, very, long shower.

The first time I'd taken Calvin up on his offer to critique my writing, I'd dutifully followed his request to write about my most embarrassing moment, an exercise I suppose he thought would get me to come out of my shell and become a more authentic writer. I wrote about a date I had in high school that went horribly awry when my father came in the room, just as my date and I were, um, getting to know each other.

We met at our usual lunch spot. I was anxious to hear his thoughts.

"Your grammar's good," he said, "but anyone could have written this."

"How can you say that, Calvin!" I was practically screeching. "This story was so painful to write!"

"I can't even tell if you were actually screwing the guy," Calvin said, taking a sip of iced tea. I didn't speak to Calvin for a long time after that. Clearly here was someone who didn't understand nuance, or, for that matter, maturity.

But alas, here I was, several years, several jobs, later, bringing Calvin up to speed on my life, my exploits, my failures, my embarrassments. Somehow, sharing them, while not necessarily vindicating me, lightened my load.

I hadn't been working with Calvin for over a year. I enjoyed the people at my new job, but not the work. Funny, I was doing exactly what I had signed on to do, what I knew I could do, but I was starting to perceive that it wasn't what I'd wanted to do. Every job in my career has been about filling someone else's need. To me, getting jobs was tantamount to having a bag of tricks. I could pull any combination of delightful qualifications, based on the hiring manager's mood and what I'd read about the company's culture. But in the end I'd felt more like a well-qualified weather vane than anything else. I could point anywhere, but the swinging was making me dizzy.

In a previous life I wrote for magazines, and I wanted to freelance—or more accurately, to write—again, but the thought of starting up the old engine of eighty pitches a day seemed daunting to me. Plus, when I wrote professionally, editors often tweaked my original ideas so many times that creating an article seemed more like origami than like personal expression. I'd gotten into a rut of making my work marketable but not unique, and certainly not worth a second look.

I made sure that employment would be on the agenda for my next lunch with Calvin. Surely he knew someone in his vast and powerful network who could help me find a new job, one that, this time, didn't make me doubt my sanity. He didn't give me quite what I was looking for, but, as I was to discover, he gave me more than I ever thought I needed: one of his portals to success.

"Why don't you start a blog?" Calvin said. I thought back to all those links to his little Web site he used to send me by e-mail. A site for people with too much time on their hands.

"That's so Valley," was my retort. "I want to get back into publishing."

"A blog will get you back into your writing, and you can test your content on people, see if they bite."

I started my blog with the most commercial of intentions—to make it back to the dog-eat-Manolo Blahniks print publishing world. Reading my first few posts feels like being on a first date, enduring someone who's strategically charming and excessively careful. I picked all-too-obvious subjects, namely reality TV shows. (Incidentally, I wrote a post about the pathetically sad show *Surreal Reality* the first weekend my blog was in existence; it still generates traffic on my site, as anyone Googling Bridgitte Nielsen can attest.) Mission seemingly accomplished.

And yet my mission wasn't accomplished. I felt like my blog was a one-sided conversation. I received very little feedback, except from my Mom, who, as anyone who reads my blog knows, stamps nearly every post I write with some comment exclaiming how proud she is of me. Calvin told me that I needed to be patient. Hell, he had set up an aggregator blog that pulled the posts off blogs he read onto his site, requiring no work on his part. Over an incubation period of three years he now received daily traffic in the thousands.

"Just think of how much more traffic you'll get just because you try," he said.

I wanted thousands! I wanted adoration. I was, you could say, like every other freaking product marketer on the planet, trying too hard. I needed an edge of some sort; I needed to be different from the others. As with all the other lessons I'd learned about authenticity, I'd learn this one unwittingly, yet inevitably, through an inauthentic urge that could not be quelled through any other means than by being real. In the end, authenticity really isn't a choice; it's the only way.

To me, getting jobs was tantamount to having a bag of tricks. I could pull any combination of delightful qualifications, based on the hiring manager's mood and what I'd read about the company's culture.

Mind you: I didn't suddenly decide one day to be authentic. I had simply given up my need to be "on," to sell myself. If I went to my computer feeling gross, then gosh-darnit, I'd let the scant few who happened to bump into my blog know it. Instead of trying to produce content, I simply translated the thoughts, the impulses that were already there. Initially this was a painful process; I would question myself, "Did I actually have that thought, or was that thought thunk in an attempt to be authentic?" But the more I wrote, the less I cared. The Web suddenly became a transparent medium through which the contents in my brain—the chatter, the anxieties, and, lo and behold, the opinions were transmitted, intact. It was around this time that I generated readers, not just traffic.

A few months into my blogging experiment, Calvin and I met for lunch. I missed our daily chats from back when we worked together; I also missed the free technical support. Calvin, as I mentioned, left the tech media company a long while back, but he was hardly struggling. Once his "network" got news of his free agency he had a full roster of consulting projects; he even had to turn away work.

"You're working hard, it seems," I said to him.

"It doesn't feel like work," Calvin said. "It feels like I've finally answered a knock at the door."

I understood how he felt. Blogging had opened a customized world for me, one that was full of possibilities, and one that didn't require me to guess what it wanted. I couldn't remember where I'd stashed my modular set of résumés, one for writing, one for project management, one for business development, and so on. The proof was in the disclosure. People saw where I was coming from and then asked if I would like to tag along on their projects. I imagined it worked that way for corporations as well—a Web site served as a reference, but the blog invited the inquiry.

I said to Calvin, "It occurs to me: It's not how much you spin but how much you share that earns you points these days."

Calvin shrugged; I tried to ignore the glob of ketchup in his beard. "Yeah, sure. . . . " he said, looking off into space. "That sounds good."

FROM THE EDITOR

I originally met Jory through fellow *More Space* writer Evelyn. I was thinking about another one of my crazy ideas (don't ask) and needed a few sci-fi writers (like I said, don't ask). Sci-fi isn't Jory's bag, but we stayed in touch. In reading Jory's work, you find a personal quality that is rare in business writing. I can't tell you how happy I am to have Jory as a part of this project. You may have seen her lead story in the May 2005 issue of *Fast Company*. Even if you didn't, I can assure you that you will be seeing a lot more of her. Jory is living out her dreams near the Golden Gate Bridge in San Francisco.

In Her Own Words . . .

What is it about your essay topic that made you want to write this chapter in *More Space*?

"All paths of growth—personal, professional, spiritual—lead to authenticity. So many people segment their values—they are good to family but horrible to work with, or vice versa. Or they would never steal from someone, but they act as though stealing resources from people or countries for economic gain is in effect OK. The more

Jory's blog:
www.jorydesjardins.com

Jory's favorite blogs:
www.tompeters.com

www.communicatrix.com

evelynrodriguez.typepad.com

Recommended reading:

The Naked Truth: A Working Woman's Manifesto on Business and What Really Matters
by Margaret Heffernan

Re-imagine!
by Tom Peters

The Alchemist
by Paul Coelho

authentic you are, the more your values line up across the board. You cannot become more authentic in your relationships and not have it affect your business life. Authenticity is all-powerful. And I'm a fairly power-driven person. ;-)"

Breakthrough Experiences

by Lisa Haneberg

Breakthrough thinking is an art and craft, fueled by an inquiring spirit and abundant experience.

—David Perkins

I have been fascinated with breakthrough experiences, which I am calling BKEs, for about ten years. That's when I began noticing the triggers and levers I could pull to experience a breakthrough. The thought of being able to send goals into high gear—of being able to trigger a breakthrough—is intoxicating, don't you think? Breakthroughs look and feel unique to the person and situation, but we can learn a lot by examining the moments before, during, and after a BKE. Here are four real examples of breakthrough moments:

Lou was not listening to a word Angela was saying. He couldn't, his mind was racing too fast. Something she had said earlier gave him an idea. "Of course, it's so logical, why didn't I think of this earlier." Bouncing from his chair, he thanked Angela and trotted on to think through the details. The meeting in five minutes would have to wait.

Stephanie felt excited, scared, and passionate the moment she crystallized what she wanted to do with her life. The insights had been building in conversations over several days. Then it happened. The thoughts and ideas came together, leaving her feeling like she had reached a mountaintop. A week before she lacked ideas and seemed stuck. Now full of passion and drive, she saw a compelling new possibility. "Can I do this?"

A rush of anger, denial, and embarrassment washed over Jean, "How dare that woman stand up in the middle of the seminar and say that my head and heart were obviously not focused on the class." But the woman was right, and as Jean stood there, after feeling vulnerable and exposed, she tapped into her desire to learn from the experience. Feeling thankful, powerful, and free, she watched the circle of seminar participants transform from empty nameless faces into partners. She was seeing them, and the day, through new eyes.

The group's sudden progress energized and excited Joseph. Several attempts to help improve his team's dialogue had failed. On the way to the meeting room, Joseph was ready to try again, but his hope was waning. Then he'd thought, "It's amazing how the right questions in the right context can enliven the conversation!"

Lou, Stephanie, Jean, and Joseph each experienced a breakthrough. Although their circumstances were different, each felt a sudden thrust of progress and forward movement. Those who experience and recognize breakthroughs know these moments are special. BKEs are like the rush of a turbo engine or the joy of a mountaintop epiphany.

BKEs help people produce results. Those who benefit from frequent BKEs enjoy more successful, exciting, and satisfying lives. Some people attribute BKEs to luck or chance. Although luck may play a small role in producing a BKE, it is more the result of being in the right places at the right times, doing the right things.

I can trace most of my major successes to one or more BKEs, and I want to learn new ways to increase the likelihood and frequency of breakthroughs. As a management trainer and coach, I have worked with hundreds of managers and find they often fall into one of two categories:

- Those who are willing and excited to try new approaches and who quickly experience BKEs.

- Those who are reluctant to change their routines although they hope for better results.

Some managers fall somewhere in the middle, but most do not. It is fun to work with the first group because significant progress can occur quickly. It's exciting. The second group takes more work, but the rewards are sweeter. I have seen several managers have ah-ha moments about ah-ha experiences. When that light bulb goes on it is like they have stepped into a whole new world.

This essay addresses both of these audiences. For the first group—the flexible and coachable types—each section has tips and ideas ready to implement right away. For the second, more change averse group, supporting material and examples help explain the concepts. The essay also speaks to me! Every time I read, refer to, edit, or discuss the topic I am reminding myself of the steps I could be taking to experience my next BKE.

My background material comes from various sources:

- A short survey I conducted with a small group

- Several books I researched (see recommended reading list at the end of this essay) and have quoted throughout these pages

- Past experiences and observations

- Beliefs and ideas developed over my career

- Discussions about breakthroughs

My goal? To improve our lives.

One of the first steps in implementing creativity at the personal level is to review your options of life contexts and then start thinking about strategies for making the best choice come true.

—Mihaly Csikszentmihalyi

DEFINING THE BREAKTHROUGH EXPERIENCE

The term breakthrough means different things to different people. Some reserve the word for scientific discoveries and efforts worthy of the Nobel Prize. Others believe they have BKEs many times a week. I prefer to take a broad and permissive view, defining a breakthrough as

- A moment when someone receives an insight, ah-ha, idea, cognitive snap (relative to the preceding time period), or epiphany

- Progress experienced by an individual or small group

- A discontinuous positive change, or a leap forward in thinking, action, or results

- A change, small or large, that involves an acceleration of progress or sudden insight (that is, transformative rather than incremental change)

Adopting this view of breakthroughs helps generate them. If I thought a breakthrough as something rare, elusive, and unlikely, I would not experience as many!

In *Archimedes' Bathtub*, David Perkins writes, "The breakthrough transforms one's mental or physical world in a generative way." BKEs are distinct from most continuous improvement efforts. The BKE jumps the tracks of sequential thinking to create a step change in results. Something now exists that did not exist before. There's clarity, where there was little or none before. An opportunity is realized. We have jumped onto a new path. BKEs are important and beneficial. They can zoom our results to new strata in ways that continuous improvement cannot. How? The graph in Figure 1 shows the difference between BKEs and continuous improvements.

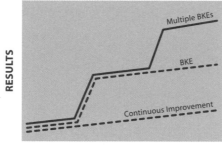

Figure 1. Breakthrough Progress

At work, home, and play, both BKEs and continuous improvement efforts are important and valuable. Some goals and problems lend themselves to a continuous improvement, step-by-step approach; others do not. If you want something big to happen, you need to generate a BKE. BKEs are also the best way to remedy being stuck or stalled. Here are the major differences between breakthroughs and continuous improvement:

FEATURE	BKEs	CONTINUOUS IMPROVEMENT
Speed	Fast	Slow, methodical
Type of progress	Skipped steps, a leap forward, discontinuous change	Incremental steps
Energy production	Enlivening, energizing	Moderate or no energy improvement
Uses	Creating new and successful possibilities in a short period of time	General ongoing business or personal growth
	Solving problems by changing the context	Solving problems within a context
	Establishing new momentum	Continuing current momentum
	Starting something new	Building a craft or practice with a long-term commitment (such as yoga, woodworking, law)
	Solving nagging problems that have not responded to other efforts	

Optimal success requires both continuous improvement methods and breakthrough thinking. The BKE offers the benefits of creating excitement, energy, and significant progress.

MAPPING THE PERSONAL BREAKTHROUGH EXPERIENCE

Some people report having BKEs often, while others believe BKEs are rare—*even if they define them in terms similar to mine.* Are the differences a matter of description? Or do some people have more breakthroughs? If the latter is true, why do these differences exist?

To further understand the BKE, I asked a group of a dozen people to complete a short survey about a recent BKE. The survey included the following questions:

1. Summarize, in just a sentence or two, a recent breakthrough you have experienced.

2. Why do you consider this a breakthrough moment?

3. Describe where you were, the number of people involved, and what you were doing when the breakthrough occurred.

4. Describe how you were feeling when you experienced the breakthrough.

5. Describe the few moments that preceded the breakthrough—what was happening and how were you feeling?

6. Describe the few moments that followed the breakthrough—what was happening and how were you feeling?

7. Was there a particular statement, question, or action that triggered the breakthrough?

8. How often would you say you experience breakthroughs?

    a. Not very often, it's a rarity

    b. Occasionally

    c. Regularly

    d. Very often

9. Describe what you mean by your response to question #8.

Please note that this is not a scientific survey. The survey questions provided a structure that respondents used to describe a recent BKE. It was interesting to read the variety of responses! The examples at the beginning of this essay came from the surveys (with names changed for privacy).

I asked respondents to read my definition of a BKE before taking the survey and requested they answer the questions with this definition in mind. I wanted to remove or minimize variances based on different definitions of breakthroughs. For example, if someone had a personal definition of a breakthrough as being something worthy of a Nobel Prize, they would likely report a lower number of BKEs than the person who saw every ah-ha as a BKE.

The survey asked respondents how they felt before, during, and after a BKE. Here is a summary of the results:

Before BKE	During BKE	After BKE
People reported feeling edgy, passive, and dissatisfied.	People reported feeling stimulated, active, focused on possibility.	People reported feeling relieved, at peace, optimistic.
Other descriptors:	**Other descriptors:**	**Other descriptors:**
• Stagnant • Unimportant • Dispassionate • Empty of ideas • Frustrated • Defensive	• Angry • Curious • Frustrated • Excited • Scared • Timid	• Full of zeal • Full of enjoyment • Satisfied • Excited • Engaged • Relieved

Although not unexpected, the results lead to a few observations:

- Uneasiness and dissatisfaction preceded most BKEs.

- Although not reflected in this chart, most BKEs occurred while in conversation with others (verbal or written).

- BKEs generated both a positive feeling and an occasional burst of adrenaline fear (the "oh shit, now what?" feeling).

- Immediately after a BKE, most felt a sense of relief and peace, even if they were still excited, buzzing, or reeling.

Many breakthroughs are preceded by a seemingly inactive period.
—David Perkins

I describe BKEs as a single moment, but they can also occur over a short period, like a day or two. I remember a very powerful BKE (or BKE sequence) I had that occurred over the weekend course that launched my writing career. Writing and publishing a book, or books, had been a dream since childhood. Looking back, it is an unlikely goal since I suffered from ADD and mild dyslexia and was not a very good reader (and therefore not a very good writer). Even so, I coveted books that I rarely read, buying them at garage sales with my allowance. As I grew up, attended college, and built my career, writing a book was always something in the back of my mind that I wanted to do. While living in New Mexico, I quit my corporate job to write. The problem was that I had no idea how the publishing industry worked or that it was a long and difficult process to get published. After a few months, I set the dream aside and got another real job to pay the bills.

The desire, perhaps need, to write a book did not go away. Finally, I decided to figure out what I needed to know to get a book published. I found and signed up for a two-day class on how to write a nonfiction book proposal. A well-known editor and book doctor, Elizabeth Lyon, taught the class. Over the course of the two days my synapses fired nonstop and I had epiphany after epiphany. I found out what I needed to do, who I needed to talk to, and my next steps. In my mind, I had imagined a Himalaya-sized mountain to climb, but I was wrong. I did what Elizabeth said (took the coaching), completed a thorough book proposal, and was able to get a great agent—and he got a publishing contract for my book. I also had several breakthroughs about the content of the book while I was writing and refining the book proposal. For example, I can still remember the day that my thoughts and questions led to the idea of targeting the book to middle managers. The concept just clicked and I was in high gear again.

This example includes several BKEs:

The moment I decided to take a class and when I found and signed up for the class. Then I experienced several smaller BKEs throughout the weekend course, and the course itself was a huge BKE—a significant shift in my focus and actions. And several other BKEs occurred during the creation of the book proposal.

The result? My first book, *High Impact Middle Management*, was published in January 2005!

My point is that BKEs may occur in a second or stretch across several days. The BKEs that I experienced occurred because of the steps I took to create them. It's not magic and anyone can do it.

Another important point: Don't waste BKEs by failing to build on them. Although my survey did not ask this question, I was able to glean from the responses (and other examples I have observed) that the overall impact of a breakthrough depends on how we react to it. The total benefit of the BKE depends on follow-up.

- High benefit: Sense of urgency, in action, building on the progress from the BKE.
- Good benefit: Positive, content with progress afforded by BKE.
- Low benefit: Positive, but not in action any longer. The progress from the BKE stalled or was lost.

As with many things in business and life, follow-up is important. I am most attracted and intrigued by the human capacity to build on and produce additional BKEs (like my book proposal example). The people who can do this are regarded as lucky. Luck has little to do with it, however.

So if you are ready, let's explore what facilitates breakthroughs and what gets in their way.

BKE CATALYSTS

BKEs occur in various circumstances, but often have similar catalysts—conditions that precede and facilitate them. To better understand BKE catalysts, I examined breakthrough research, survey responses, and other individual accounts. The resulting list is not exhaustive, of course—potential BKE catalysts come in many forms, and they will vary by individual.

These are the most common BKE catalysts:

- Dissonance experiences
- Taking action
- Deep thinking
- Coached nudges
- Making requests
- Changing or realigning the context
- Incubation or time away
- Practice, practice, practice

Dissonance Experiences

We all need an occasional "whack on the head" to shake us out of routine patterns, to force us to re-think our problems, and to stimulate us to ask the questions that may lead to other right answers.

—Roger Von Oech

Some BKEs happen when people experience cognitive dissonance.* Failed attempts, rejections, and embarrassment may cause us to question what we are doing and explore new possibilities. While we do not hope for failure to occur, we can use these experiences to progress and enjoy BKEs. If we take on a defensive or uncoachable stance, a BKE is unlikely.

There's being wrong or insightfully wrong.

—David Perkins

Significant anomalies can also cause dissonance. Exploring the reasons and origins for the anomaly will yield fresh ideas and new perspectives, and perhaps a BKE. Dissonance results in a shock and a jerk into a new paradigm or reality. Fear of failure, fear of not being good enough, can hold us back. When we make a decisive break with the

*Dissonance: A condition of conflict or anxiety resulting from inconsistency between one's beliefs and one's actions or results.

past, we open the possibility of a breakthrough.

Breakthrough begins with estrangement.
—Charles David Axelrod

Taking Action

Are you in earnest? Seize this very minute! Boldness has genius, power, and magic in it. Only engage, and then the mind grows heated. Begin, and then the work will be completed.
—John Anster

Getting into action is a great way to create momentum and put your goals and intentions into the world—an important step in BKEs. Many of the BKE catalysts are also forms of taking action. Taking action means trying something new, moving before you're pushed, or doing what you've been putting off. This is one of my strongest BKE catalysts. My progress suffers when I wait and react to things that happen to me.

Deep Thinking

With an eye made quiet by the power of harmony, and the deep power of joy, we see into the life of things.
—William Wordsworth

Some people use mental retreats to generate new ideas, refocus, and tap into their goals. Whether away, at home, or at the office, deep thinking includes mountaintop thinking,* playing around with ideas, talking to oneself, and noticing things in a new way.

*Mountaintop thinking: Being with your thoughts in a place that is relaxing, inspiring, and conducive to concentration. Often associated with sitting on a rock on the top of a mountain and contemplating the meaning of life.

Coached Nudges

Your luck depends on the actions of other people and whether or not they decide to help you get what you want.
—Marc Myers

Among the survey respondents, coached nudges outnumbered other BKE catalysts in the roster of reported BKEs. In fact, most breakthroughs occurred following worthwhile conversations of various sorts: e-mail exchanges, blogging, phone calls, and live discussions.

Creativity does not happen inside people's heads, but in the interaction between a person's thoughts and a sociocultural context.
—Mihaly Csikszentmihalyi

When a peer, friend, manager, or stranger says just what we need to hear, it is a special gift. When we are open to them, coached nudges can help bring on BKEs. People differ on whether they seek and welcome coaching from others. Those who are highly coachable will receive and use more coached nudges and experience more BKEs.

Conversations are powerful tools. I believe that reality is socially constructed.** Change the conversation and you can change the reality. By communicating our goals, intentions, ideas and hopes, we deploy a support system that can make a world of difference. When managers lament that their careers are not going according to their hopes, I ask, "what do you want to have happen and who knows about your goals?" Often, they have neither defined nor communicated their goals adequately.

**Social constructionism: Theory of how interactions and social practices contribute to the way in which people define what is real or has meaning.

Making Requests

Great things are only possible with outrageous requests.

—Thea Alexander

Making requests is perhaps the easiest and fastest way to produce BKEs. Mahatma Gandhi said, "If you don't ask, you don't get," and I believe this to be true. It is important to make requests that will make a difference and enable progress. Requests come in two types:

- Everyday requests—reasonable, modest, helpful
- Prime requests—a tad beyond what we feel to be reasonable, big, would make a significant difference if granted

Both everyday and prime requests are helpful and should be a regular part of your daily and weekly practices. The more prime requests you make, the better your chances for exciting BKEs. Prime requests will be turned down more often, but the few that are granted will have a disproportionately higher positive impact.

What I point out to people is that it's silly to be afraid that you're not going to get what you want if you ask. Because you are already not getting what you want. They always laugh about that because they realize it's so true. Without asking you already have failed, you already have nothing. What are you afraid of? You're afraid of getting what you already have! It's ridiculous! Who cares if you don't get it when you ask for it, because, before you ask for it, you don't have it anyway. So there's really nothing to be afraid of.

—Marcia Martin

I have a weekly routine that has been successful. Each week I make at least five prime requests. The more I ask, the better. I design the requests to move various goals and projects forward. I have had some amazing things happen because of my requests. Most people want to help if they can. In fact, some people will get a charge out of granting your request and may experience a BKE for themselves! A granted request creates an immediate shift in circumstances and bolsters your goals and direction. Even if only one in ten prime requests gets granted, that one request can create a new reality.

Some people feel uncomfortable making requests because they feel selfish and unworthy. If requests are well thought out and focused, they will increase our contribution and help us be more successful—this is not selfish because we owe it to the world to perform our best work possible.

Changing Or Realigning The Context

It is easier to enhance creativity by changing conditions in the environment than by trying to make people think more creatively.

—Mihaly Csikszentmihalyi

One of the most effective ways to bring about a BKE is to adjust the context.* In *The Tipping Point*, Malcolm Gladwell wrote about how the New York City crime rate plummeted in the 1990s, enabled in large part by changes made to the context. Implementing the Broken Windows theory,** they first cleaned up the graffiti on subway cars, and then stopped subway riders from jumping the turnstiles. Once the look and feel of the subway experience changed, crimes dropped.

A change in context can have a dramatic impact on our perspective and results. Changing the context might mean creating a workspace that is pleasant and relaxed. The ancient practice of feng shui seeks to align surrounding elements to the goals of each space. Even those who do not follow feng shui will likely acknowledge that a cluttered workspace often accompanies a cluttered mind.

*Context: The setting, surroundings, or circumstances of a place or concept. The context includes the environment, fixtures, contents, pace, policies, and general practices.

**Broken Windows theory: If a broken window is allowed to stay broken, passers-by will figure that no one cares and no one is in charge. Some will break more windows, and anarchy spreads out through the neighborhood. Malcolm Gladwell attributes this theory to George Kelling and James Q. Wilson.

Another example of a context change is exploring unknown surroundings to broaden thinking and perspectives. Asking a new group of people to help brainstorm solutions to a problem is a contextual change.

Strangers have a heightened capacity for rendering impartial judgments.

—Charles David Axelrod

New or unexpected external circumstances can provide the precipitating event that triggers a BKE. For example, anomalies can represent a contextual change. Those who explore anomalies are often rewarded with new insights, approaches, and BKEs.

Incubation Or Time Away

Several people said that their best thinking occurs when they take a mental break from working on a problem or goal. Watching people walk down the street can trigger an insight. Overthinking something is a real risk, and taking a break can help us forget or set aside assumptions and mental sets that might be getting in the way of progress.

It's often been suggested that something crucial happens during this time away from the problem when the thinker invests no obvious effort in pursuing it.

—David Perkins

Perhaps the human brain needs a rest and perhaps it is not resting at all. Some believe that the subconscious mind continues to work on a solution while the conscious mind focuses elsewhere. In either case, it is sometimes fruitful to take a breather!

Practice, Practice, Practice

Creativity is idiosyncratic—each person has their own way.

—Michael Ray

This catalyst comes from a conversation I had with Michael Ray, author of *The Highest Goal*. Michael emphasizes that breakthroughs are more likely to occur when you employ catalysts that work for you on a consistent basis (for example, my routine of asking requests each week). He urges everyone to find the methods that work and create a positive practice.

We also need to try new approaches, but many of us give up on methods too soon and don't reap the benefits. If you try meditation, for example, it could take days, weeks, or months to get to the place where BKEs can be generated.

The first step toward a more creative life is the cultivation of curiosity and interest, that is, the allocation of attention to things for their own sake.

—Mihaly Csikszentmihalyi

These are the most common catalysts, but you may enjoy others. For me, getting into action, making requests, and changing the context have made the greatest difference. Give each one a try!

BKE INHIBITORS

BKE catalysts improve conditions for a breakthrough. BKE inhibitors get in the way and make breakthroughs less likely. To take advantage of and have the mental energy to use BKE catalysts, we need to identify and reduce the number of BKE inhibitors getting in our way. Unless you are superhuman, you will recognize one or more of these BKE inhibitors:

- Measure a hundred times, never cut
- Focus on logic

- Scarcity mind-set
- Fear
- Self-fulfilling prophecy
- No room at the (mental) inn
- Schools of thought
- Hard work
- Be careful what you ask for

Of course, many of these BKE inhibitors can also be good habits in some situations. For example, being logical is often desirable—but a preoccupation with all things logical can get in the way.

Measure A Hundred Times, Never Cut

You've heard the saying, "Measure twice, cut once," right? That's good advice, but some people take it too far. Often called paralysis by analysis, this BKE inhibitor gets in the way because, while analysis is a kind of action, too much analysis precludes forward movement. This is particularly the case for analysis that does not move outside the context (a BKE catalyst). How do you know when you have gone too far? You need a new approach when your progress has slowed or stalled and people are losing patience and interest.

Ask yourself—Do I really need to know this? What is the worst thing that could happen if I go ahead and make a decision? Will it be the end of the world if we need to adjust the course down the road a bit?

Focus On Logic

Logic, like whiskey, loses its beneficial effect when taken in too large quantities.
—Lord Dunsany

Breakthroughs, by definition, come as a surprise or something unexpected. Therefore, if you only do what is logical and familiar, you will reduce the number of possible BKEs. Progress follows a path paved by logical and not-so-logical developments. When collecting and considering ideas and approaches, don't worry about whether something is logical. You'll have time to question the viability of the idea later, after you've played with the concepts a bit.

Breakthrough insights do not typically require a great deal of reasoning.
—David Perkins

As a BKE inhibitor, logic is similar to paralysis by analysis because it stems from a need or comfort with data or information. Think about the progress you have enjoyed. Could you have predicted and planned how it occurred? For many situations, the answer will be no. To help you generate and consider a variety of ideas and options (not just the logical ones), ask more open-ended questions and get input from a wider variety of people. Resolve to give new approaches a try, starting small if that works better for you.

Scarcity Mind-set

I see this one a lot. Some people are not really in tune with what's possible. They try one idea and then get discouraged if it does not work. They think it wrong to make requests to move goals forward. They live in a mental paradigm that is focused on limits and reasons not to branch out and be creative. Their socially constructed reality is one of scarce resources and possibilities. Individuals with this perspective drastically reduce their opportunities for BKEs. It is a constant battle to help folks with a scarcity mind-set venture out and explore new ideas. In my experience, they are not likely to do this on their own, either. So if you know of someone affected by a scarcity mind-set, try offering them coaching and support.

The universe is full of magical things patiently waiting for our wits to grow sharper.
—Eden Phillpotts

I am using "they" a lot here because this BKE inhibitor is not typically a problem for me. In fact, I tend to err on the other side, thinking anything is possible and everything is available. That said, I have worked with several people who suffer from a scarcity mind-set. One person in particular, I will call him Chris, was brilliant but lived a life well below his potential. His social makeup, or DNA, or something, was hardwired to see his world as half empty and leaking. What worked for him? When I would share examples of employing a BKE catalyst and making something happen, he could get inspired and I could see him trying a new idea and getting in action for a couple of days. When his efforts worked, his view would be one of abundance for a bit longer. Eventually, he would go back to the scarcity mind-set. So for Chris, the solution is frequent and positive examples of alternative approaches that inspire him to get more involved in the game of life.

Fear

Anything I've ever done that ultimately was worthwhile . . . initially scared me to death.
—Betty Bender

Fear affects us all at some point. When we let fear get in the way, we eliminate many possibilities. I am not suggesting that you become reckless. Most fears have nothing to do with impending danger; they're rooted in a need to be right or save face.

The fear of being wrong is the prime inhibitor of the creative process.
—Jean Bryant

In his classic *How to Win Friends and Influence People*, Dale Carnegie suggests that 99 percent of our worries don't come true and therefore we should not let them get in the way. I believe this is true and try to remind myself of it when I get into a worrisome mode. I know that if I am preoccupied with fear, I am not emotionally available to progress or experience a BKE. And I want BKEs!

This is the BKE inhibitor that gives me the most trouble. I have found that changing my self talk to ask questions like, "What's the downside?" or "What are you really afraid of—and does that matter?" works best for me. I try to distinguish and separate my fears of pain and setback from fears about not looking good or right.

Self-fulfilling Prophecy

Confidence is contagious. So is lack of confidence.
—Michael O'Brien

The self-fulfilling prophecy* can be helpful or unhelpful. When we assume that we will fail and never experience a breakthrough, we are often right. Our failure occurs not because that was the likely outcome, however, but because we tuned our brains for defeat. My best friend suffers from this and it is a shame. He is brilliant, dedicated, and hardworking, but he sees his world as small and defeating. He has suffered from this failure mind-set most of his life. All is not lost and there is hope! He does have days when he entertains and takes on more positive and compelling expectations.

*Self-fulfilling prophecy, or Pygmalion effect: Once we establish an expectation, even if it isn't accurate, we (and others) tend to act in ways that are consistent with that expectation. Our expectations often determine what becomes reality.

Confidence is a lot of this game or any game. If you don't think you can, you won't.
—Jerry West

To combat the negative self-fulfilling prophecy, we need to pay attention to and reprogram our destructive self-talk. By acknowledging the power of the self-fulfilling prophecy, we can create and employ a more positive model. This can occur over time or instantly. Just a couple of days ago, I was meeting someone for coffee—someone who could potentially make a significant positive difference to my business and livelihood. As I was waiting, my thoughts were small and negative. I was slumping in my chair and I am sure I looked unremarkable. As I saw the person enter the coffee shop, I noticed who I was being and quickly told my mind to snap out of it and be magnificent. The meeting went as well as could be expected!

No Room At The (Mental) Inn

The fact is that there are real limits to how many things a person can attend to at the same time.

—Mihaly Csikszentmihalyi

Attention is a limited resource. At any given time, we have just so much information we can process. I think most of us know this, and yet do we carve out time to think and create new ideas? I am guilty of this in spades—doing too much. There is a difference between making time and taking time. When we make time, we are adding burdens to the day and may push ourselves beyond our mental capacity. When we take time, by contrast, we are setting time aside in the day to focus on our goal, not adding to the workday.

When we have no room at the mental inn, we are not available to receive the information that could result in a BKE. We may be brilliant, but if we are always distracted, we will not produce our best ideas or listen well.

In other words, when we are feeling burned out and overwhelmed, we are less likely to experience breakthroughs! The solution is simple, but hard to do—do less, take on fewer projects, take a mental break.

Schools Of Thought

We have certain beliefs and assumptions about how things ought to go. When our schools of thought narrow our range of possibilities, they get in the way of BKEs. Here are several great quotes from the same source, *Studies in Intellectual Breakthroughs* by Charles David Axelrod:

> We do not recognize our natural tendency to omit/limit/categorize info and reject thoughts and ideas counter to the current paradigm.

> Other side of membership—its narrowing and confining capacity.

> It is the community that breakthrough must break through.

> Ordinary conversations cannot be authentic speech, for what is merely a fragment is presented as the whole.

> Estrangement is a necessary ingredient of discourse.

This BKE inhibitor relates to the BKE catalyst of changing the context. Breakthroughs often involve experiencing a paradigm shift. In his *Archimedes' Bathtub*, David Perkins shares an example of how our mental sets shape and inhibit our thinking. A group of people was asked to draw a picture of what aliens from outer space might look like. Not surprisingly, most people drew the stereotypical large-headed beast with arms, legs, and eyes.

People find it difficult to escape from templates well established in their minds. . . . Breakthrough thinking involves breaking through unhelpful mental sets.

—David Perkins

To combat this BKE inhibitor, we need to expand our influences and conversations. Invite a diversity of people to the dialogue. Try a new approach. Attend a class taught and attended by people you do not know.

Hard Work

The truth is that hard work doesn't get us what we want nearly as often as most people think.

—Marc Myers

It is interesting to sit back, take a look at our goals, and ask what we could do that would make the greatest difference in facilitating success. The answer may not be to work hard. Big breakthroughs may occur because of small actions. These are just some of the potential concerns with hard work:

- We may exhaust our mental capacity.
- We can spend lots of energy and time without making progress.
- Working hard in one direction will prevent us from considering other contexts.
- When we are working hard at something, we are less able to view the circumstances objectively.

I am not suggesting that working hard is a bad thing. But if your progress toward your goals is unsatisfactory, you should assess whether your efforts are unintentionally getting in the way of a BKE.

Hard work just isn't very efficient.

—Marc Myers

If you have been trying the same approach, working in the same direction, for a long time, it is unlikely that working harder in the same direction is going to help. Ask yourself, "Is this working?" If the answer is no, then perhaps you are trying too hard doing the wrong things.

Be Careful What You Ask For!

The more important a call or action is to our soul's evolution, the more resistance we will feel toward pursuing it.

—Steven Pressfield

Resistance is a type of fear, but it is worth calling out as a separate BKE inhibitor. Many of us don't go for our goals with gusto because we are afraid of what will happen if we get what we ask for. Why? We are vulnerable when we play full-out. What if our best is not good enough? We all experience resistance and respond to it differently. The important question is whether we let resistance sap us of our power and the energy needed to build a life we love.

BKE inhibitors grind us down every day. Looking down the list, we can quickly identify those that are most troublesome. To experience and enjoy more BKEs, minimize the number and frequency of BKE inhibitors.

PRODUCING MORE BKEs

My purpose here is to explore the nature of BKEs so as to promote more and better breakthroughs. So how does the information shared thus far lead to that goal? I see it as following this formula:

$$MS + H - I = BKEs$$

(That is, a BKE mind-set plus enabling habits minus inhibitors will increase BKEs.)

I hope it is clear that producing BKEs is influenced by how we think, what we do, and the people we involve. Anyone can learn how to improve the odds of a BKE by focusing on these elements.

The BKE Mind-set

The BKE mind-set is a set of beliefs that enable more breakthroughs. I call this becoming BKE enabled. By taking on these beliefs, your head and heart will be primed for amazing things to happen. A word of caution: you may have to remind yourself of these beliefs often. For example, I am entrenched with this topic as I sit and write, yet I need reminders! I had a tough day and had to remind myself several times that a negative or grumpy state of mind would only make my situation worse. It can be tough; sometimes it's tempting to want to play the victim. Here's the rub: nobody can be the victim and still turn things around for the better. I know that if I'm going to help myself, I need to shift my paradigm to a BKE mind-set.

Here are several beliefs* that make up the BKE mind-set:

* A note about beliefs: Beliefs need not be correct to be helpful. For example, "I won't get what I don't request" might not be true 100 percent of the time. We do get some things that we have not asked for from others. Even so, taking on this belief is helpful. When selecting beliefs, the most important question to ask is, "Will this assumption serve my goals well?"

- Playing the victim is not helpful.
- Sometimes I need to be hit on the head with failure so I can learn from dissonance.
- If things are not moving, I need to get into action.
- I need to share my goals and intentions with others in a position to support them. The more my goals are in conversation, the better.
- Breakthroughs often occur during a paradigm shift. I should seek and welcome paradigm shifts.
- To keep the capacity for insight and breakthrough, I need to avoid draining my mental batteries.
- The more coachable I am, the better the coaching I will receive. The right coaching can make a huge difference.
- I won't get what I don't request.
- "Negativity and bragging lead to failure." (Marc Myers)
- "Fight off feelings of envy at all costs." (Marc Myers)
- "Without awe, life becomes routine." (Mihaly Csikszentmihalyi)
- "Problems tend to be remembered simply by virtue of being worked on." (David Perkins)
- "Having a constant flow of breakthroughs is achieving the highest goal. They are moments of grace." (Michael Ray)

You get the picture. If you want to change results, adjust your beliefs so they support your goals. This may seem difficult, but it does not have to be. Try creating your own list of beliefs that you feel will serve your goals. Review them every morning and every time you feel you're experiencing a setback until you do not need to do so any longer. If you want feedback on your list of beliefs, e-mail them to me at lhaneberg@gmail.com; I would be happy to offer my thoughts. Here is one of the biggest self-fulfilling prophecies of all: Those who say it is hard to adjust beliefs will always be right. But beliefs can be very easy to adjust—and when you see it this way, it will be this way.

Here's one last belief that I created myself. I repeat it when I am having a bad day:

> Woe is me, pity parties, and whining are of no use! I cannot possibly turn this day around with this attitude—snap out of it, your life is great!

And it works . . .

BKE Habits

When something strikes a spark of interest, follow it.
—Mihaly Csikszentmihalyi

BKE habits are the actions that naturally follow when we take on the BKE mind-set. I have always said, "Great managers do what others don't." This thought applies to many aspects of life. Those in action and engaged will experience more BKEs than those who sit back and wait for something to happen.

Often it is the second answer, which, although offbeat or unusual, is exactly what you need to solve a problem in an innovative way.
—Roger von Oech

A list of BKE habits:

- Get in action and stay in action.
- Collect many ideas from various sources.
- Make at least five requests related to your goals every week.
- Broadly share your goals and intentions.
- Change your context as needed (if you are stalled, it's needed).
- Master the art of great dialogue.
- Snap yourself out of funks, poor moods, or bouts of frustration—quickly.
- Take time (not make time) to reflect, relax, and create new ideas.
- Seek BKEs without feeling entitled to them.
- Ask for and appreciate opposing views and contrary thought.
- Try new things.
- Play at work and at home, and not just in formal leisure activities.
- Feed your curiosities!

Practice these BKE habits and you will experience more breakthroughs and enjoy greater success.

Asking a crucial question figures centrally in the cognitive snap.
—David Perkins

CONCLUSION

When a breakthrough occurs, it is like magic. A special surge of positive energy and optimism runs through our veins and something happens.

Something happens. . . . Reality shifts and new possibilities emerge.

BKEs are gifts. They put the life in life.

I hope this essay will help you improve your life by producing more BKEs!

<aside>
Lisa's blog:
www.managementcraft.com

Lisa's favorite blogs:
www.ottmarliebert.com/blog
headrush.typepad.com
evelynrodriguez.typepad.com

Recommended reading:

The Art of Possibility
by Rosamund Stone Zander and Benjamin Zander

Creativity
by Mihaly Csikszentmihalyi

The Highest Goal
by Michael Ray

Harvard Business Review on Breakthrough Thinking
by Teresa Amabile, et al.

Studies in Intellectual Breakthrough
by Charles Alexrod

The Elements of Learning
by James Banner and Harold Cannon

Change Your Mind, Change Your World
by Richard Gillett

The Power of Positive Choices
by Gail McMeekin

How to Make Luck
by Marc Meyers

Archimedes' Bathtub
by David Perkins

The War of Art: Break Through the Blocks and Win Your Inner Creative Battles
by Steven Pressfield
</aside>

FROM THE EDITOR

What I find most interesting about Lisa is the passion she has for so many different things. She has written extensively on management (*H.I.M.M.—High Impact Middle Management: Solutions for Today's Busy Managers*). She also helps companies hire talent that matches the needs of their organizations. And now, with this essay as a primer, she is working on a book called *2 Weeks 2 a Breakthrough*. Lisa is a stone's throw away from the Washington State Ferry Docks (in Seattle), but you might find her heart in the southwest.

In Her Own Words . . .

What is it about your essay topic that made you want to write this chapter in *More Space*?

"I have done a lot of working with breakthroughs and found that it was making its way into my books and blog posts. The thought of doing some research and creating a meaty piece about breakthroughs was a next logical step. Breakthroughs are what I am most interested in right now. Having them, facilitating them, learning about them, and enjoying them."

72

Simple Ideas, Lightly Held

----

by Johnnie Moore

Life is complex, but it isn't complicated.

I'm going to explain what I mean by that, and why it means that many of the rules and prescriptions in business books for how to do things need to be taken with a big pinch of salt.

Instead, I suggest relying more often on a few rules of thumb, knowing that they are not the gospel truth. Some simple ideas work really well for me and my clients. They are drawn from the world of improv (improvisational theater) and I find them highly effective in my work—which involves helping organizations develop better teamwork and creativity. I'm not going to give you an exhaustive explanation of the depths of improv; instead I'm going to introduce you to a few of its principles and invite you try them on for size.

If you're the sort that likes a bit of explanation before trying something new, continue reading. If you're more of a "learning by doing" person, you might want to skip to the section headed "Try This With A Friend". You can come back to the other bits another time.

THE DIFFERENCE BETWEEN COMPLICATED AND COMPLEX

This is what I mean when I use the word complicated:

The wiring on an aircraft is complicated. To figure out where everything goes would take a long time. But if you studied it for long enough, you could know with (near) certainty what each electrical circuit does and how to control it. The system is ultimately knowable. If understanding it is important, the effort to study it and make a detailed diagram of it would be worthwhile.

So complicated = not simple, but ultimately knowable.

Now, put a crew and passengers in that aircraft and try to figure out what will happen on the flight. Suddenly we go from complicated to complex. You could study the lives of all these people for years, but you could never know all there is to know about how they will interact. You could make some guesses, but you can never know for sure. And the effort to study all the elements in more and more detail will never give you that certainty.

So complex = not simple and never fully knowable. Just too many variables interact.

Managing humans will never be complicated. It will always be complex. So no book or diagram or expert is ever going to reveal the truth about managing people.

But don't panic. We can manage people if we stop trying too hard to get it right. We just have to live with that uncertainty and come to enjoy it.

Mihaly Csikszentmihalyi (try spelling that after a couple of beers) puts it like this in *Good Business: Leadership, Flow and the Making of Meaning:* "One of the key tasks of management is to create an organization that stimulates the complexity of those who belong to it."

Great Theory; What Does It Mean In Practice?

Think for a minute about Southwest Airlines. This is a U.S. airline that for many years has been widely recognized as much more successful and profitable than nearly all its competitors.

Southwest does not come across as a secretive company. There's a whole reality TV show revealing it, warts and all. There's not much about the way it functions that hasn't been examined and described. I'd venture to guess that most of what could be made explicit about how Southwest works has been made explicit.

So it's very interesting that almost no other airline comes anywhere close to Southwest in terms of success.

There seems to be a basic assumption, from business schools to bookstores, that success is only a matter of modeling something that works, making the process explicit, and copying it. The Southwest paradox suggests there's something fundamentally faulty in that assumption.

That's because like all human organizations Southwest is complex, not complicated. Trying to copy it would involve an impossible effort to replicate all the unknowable details of what makes it work (and there are a lot of variables . . . the market it grew up in has changed; no one can replicate the personality of its individual managers; you can't be the first to do what it does . . . and so on and on).

Lots of deep stuff is written about systems, chaos, and complexity. My own search is for simple ways of dealing with complexity—ways that don't attempt to cover all the bases but still allow us to embrace paradox and ambiguity in our decision making. This seems pretty much the essence of creative living. . . .

One of my favorite management writers, Richard Farson, says in *Management of the Absurd:*

> In organizations, as in life, human behavior is often irrational—and problems do not easily lend themselves to the simplistic answers and gimmickry offered in the myriad business "self-help" books and management training programs available today. . . .

> It is the ability to meet each situation armed not with a battery of techniques but with openness that permits a genuine response. The better managers transcend technique. Having acquired many techniques in their development as professionals, they succeed precisely by leaving technique behind.

I don't think human relationships are simple; I think they are complex. Paradoxically, I think that the best principles to follow are simple but also fuzzy and fallible. But it's much better to be approximately right than precisely wrong. It's better to contain the ambiguity and uncertainty than to live in denial of it.

As organizations grow, there's a tendency to reduce ambiguity by adding to the rule book. In part, this is a natural desire to embody the lessons of past mistakes. But the effect over time can be sclerotic.

Look at traffic lights in cities. Over time, more and more road junctions in London have been graced with traffic lights in an effort to prevent gridlock and improve traffic flow. The trouble is that although these lights may work in isolation, their cumulative effect is often to make the traffic worse. And recent experiments have shown that stripping all the lights out of a stretch of road has actually reduced congestion.

Growing From Where We Are Now

One of the biggest problems with trying to change is the reluctance to acknowledge where we are now. Southwest Airlines did not grow out of a vacuum, it arose from a whole set of circumstances unique to its location and the time in which it grew up. The company preferred Love Field over the new Dallas airport and it avoided many regulations by flying entirely within Texas in its early years.

Trying to copy a business without noticing these unrepeatable differences of context is like putting up an elaborate rococo trellis and not noticing that instead of a Russian vine, someone has planted potatoes.

And while it's fine to draw inspiration from others, we need to get better at growing from where we are now, not from where someone else is.

Not Bowling Alone

Fortunately, we don't have to grow alone. What all those success stories have in common is that they all grew from the collaboration of lots of different people. Oh, some heroes may well be involved, but they came out of the interactions of lots of different people.

So I want to set out a few simple ideas about how we can grow together without baffling ourselves with diagrams and lists of instructions. These ideas are lightly held, because as already noted, there are no universal truths about organizational life.

OK, But What Simple Ideas?

I don't know for sure what simple ideas will work best for you. But I'll share a few that work for me.

These ideas are taken from the world of improv. Actors use them to create great theater and we can use them to create . . . great theater. The sort of theater that engages staff and customers, creates a good spirit of teamwork, and deals with the unexpected with aplomb. You know, all that good stuff that seems easier to write books about than to do. . . .

These ideas resonate with my own experiences, both as a marketing guy and as a facilitator of groups and mediator of heated human disputes.

- Yes, And
- Be Affected
- Embrace Surprise

Not The Whole Truth

I didn't find it easy learning to ski. I've never been very good in classes, and I went through several hours of one-to-one instruction falling down and feeling pissed off.

I remember the point at which my instructor turned things around. He threw out this idea for my posture: imagine you are a holding a tray of champagne glasses as you move down the slope. This was a strange idea, but as soon as I tried it, something changed and suddenly I knew I was skiing with a different feeling, and on another level. As in, ooh-err instead of ouch, and sort of upright instead of horizontal.

Later, another instructor noticed I was using my poles more like an ancient tribesman spearing fish. So for a while, he took them away—helping me to learn more about balance. Later, I could go back to poles with more of a clue how to use them.

Both these interventions worked where others failed. Neither made a lot of sense as mere ideas, yet they both generated results in practice. And once they'd worked, I didn't need to cling to them rigidly. I don't normally think of champagne glasses when I'm skiing. Once you're in some kind of flow state, you're not thinking about "the rules."

You might care to think of the following ideas in the same way. Not as "the truth" about organizations or life, but more as ideas to try out and see what happens.

In the language of improv, these are offers, which you may choose to accept and build on, or to block—by stopping reading, or by generating stories about how they won't work or how some people would never do them.

TRY THIS WITH A FRIEND

Well done, you've either read all the explanations above, or you've skipped here. However you got here, welcome.

I invite you to read this section with one or more friends and colleagues, and follow some of the exercises together.

The trouble with reading books like this is that it tends to be a solitary experience. (Mind you, try writing one.) The essence of these ideas is that they are ways to create stuff together, not on our own. Also, I'd like you to learn by doing, rather than simply studying the words on the page.

So here are the instructions for a simple activity to be done with one other person (you could adapt it for more people or get them to work in pairs). My suggestion is that you try a few rounds of this activity before reading on. I think it provides a good context for the material that follows. Then again, you may be like me, and feel impatient to get to the point, in which case you might try the activity later.

Or don't play at all, see if I care.

Anyway, here it is:

Paired Drawing

I've illustrated this with two examples. Not to show you the "right" answers, but to reassure you that we're not expecting Picasso here.

The exercise is simple: you're going to draw a face, together. It won't be a familiar face (probably) but one you're making up between you.

Once you're ready, you work silently. Resist the urge to discuss the picture as it develops and don't comment on each other's ideas. (You probably won't be able to suppress laughter, though.)

Draw just one feature of a face. It's up to you what it is: it could be an ear, an eye, a nose, a tattoo, an eyebrow . . . whatever. Rule of thumb: when you lift the pen off the paper, you've finished your turn. And remember, as you're working silently, don't explain what you've drawn.

Then your partner takes the pen and draws a feature. It may be another ear or eye, or it could be something else. Whatever it is, you then get the pen and carry on. Even if you're not sure what has been drawn.

And if you don't know—don't ask! Just carry on adding features as best you can.

Keep going like this for a few turns, each adding a single feature with each turn.

When someone gets the pen and hesitates about what to do, this means the face is finished. So that person now puts down the first letter of the name of this character. Keep adding letters until someone hesitates—and then you've finished.

And again, don't comment on what your partner writes, whatever you may think!

It's a good idea to do this at least three times. It's interesting to see how the experience changes with each repetition.

I suggest you now take a few moments to reflect with your partner on what it was like to do this together.

What was it like to create something mutually? Do you sense that what you drew is different from the picture either of you might have created alone?

Did you find that what your partner did sometimes surprised you? Was some existing plan of your own for "how things should be" disrupted?

Did you sometimes find the process amusing and enjoyable? If so, what was enjoyable about it?

What did you learn about working together from doing this?

I usually find that people engage with the exercise with ease and often enthusiasm. I often ask why we play games like this with more commitment than we give to many business meetings that, in theory, are about much more important topics. (Sometimes participants think this activity is pointless—and find it hard to explain their enthusiasm.)

What you've done here, with your partner, is to create something together that neither of you controlled, though you both influenced it. You contributed your own ideas and built on the other person's. So even if your partner drew something weird, or something you didn't like, you found a way to say: *Yes, and* . . . to them. You didn't (I hope) cross their stuff out, you let yourself be affected by their contribution. And if it was odd, well, you let yourself be surprised. Pleasantly, I hope.

I use activities like this—and the others we're going to try later—to support creative thinking and teambuilding. Sometimes people use them as a warm up exercise, but I think what they show us is more profound.

A Quick Side Note About Structure And Freedom

I've run this exercise lots of times now with hundreds of people. And you know what? All the drawings are of faces and they all have names. No one (so far) has ended up drawing a map of Africa or written a limerick.

I mention this now because when some people hear about improv they predict anarchy. But improv is not anarchy; each activity has a certain amount of structure. And then within the structure, people get to explore possibility. And this is what any sane organization wants its people to be willing to do:

> to take a set of constraints and explore what is possible within them.
>
> And now back to our normal program. . . .

Congratulations. This is a microcosm of what it is to improvise.

And now for some more details.

Idea 1: Yes, And

At its simplest level, this is an injunction to stop saying "No, but" to our colleagues and instead say "Yes, and." It's not always going to work, but I've been surprised at the difference it makes when I find myself able to do this with sincerity.

No, I'm not suggesting that you simply agree with everything people say to you, so don't panic. To put this all in context, here's another simple activity you could try with a colleague.

> *What I Like . . .*
>
> Pick a subject where you'd like to generate a few creative ideas. For a warm-up, maybe choose one that's not of world-shattering importance, so that it's easy to engage with lightness. Like . . . where shall we go for lunch next time?
>
> The first person gets to make one suggestion for what you do—say, "Let's go to the staff cafeteria."
>
> The second person then says, "Yes, what I like about that idea is . . . " and then adds something they do like about it. The challenge is to find something you really like, which may take a second or two. For example "Yes, what I like about that idea is that it's a quick journey and that means we can spend more time talking."
>
> This person then continues, "And we could—" making another suggestion. For this exercise, don't worry too much about connecting to the first idea, just play. So you might say, "And we could eat the hottest curry on the menu."
>
> Back to the first person, who now continues with "Yes, what I like about that idea is . . . that as I don't eat spicy food, I get to do most of the talking!"
>
> And so on, until you decide to stop for coffee.

What this exercise may bring up:

For a lot of folks, this is great fun; they generate some wild ideas and get enthusiastic.

Others play at a slower pace but learn that they can find things to appreciate in what another person says, if they try.

And a few hate it, because (they say) it forces fake enthusiasm. That's an interesting point of view, but I don't believe the activity forces that—it's a choice that the participants make. With an effort I think it's always possible to find something to appreciate about the other's offer.

I'd observe that within the structure of this activity, people will explore what's possible and therefore come up with different styles and interpretations. That's why I tend to ask people to play games without attempting to explain what "the point is."

Anyway, some will insist on *No, but* for a *Yes, and* activity. That is always an option. Generally, I've found *Yes, and* works well for me in many more cases because most people like to be acknowledged.

The Simple Power Of Acknowledgment . . .

"Yes, and" is sometimes more about acknowledgment of the other than it is about agreement.

I think acknowledging other people's experience can be remarkably powerful, especially in situations of conflict. Yet it's something we as a race are incredibly bad at doing.

What we like to do is offer our interpretation of what someone tells us, or rush to suggestions on how to avoid having certain feelings, rather than simply acknowledging them.

Time and again, I find that when I stop and simply let someone know I've heard what they said, and the way they said it, the quality of conversation improves for both of us. And when others do it to me, the impact is similarly strong.

And I've done it for myself. I remember on September 12, 2001, I was talking to an old friend who had invited me over for lunch. I actually felt unable to leave home, suffering like many other people from the shock of the day before. And then I just said to him, "Oh, I realize I feel too afraid to go out of the door, just give me a minute or two to feel that." And after a few moments of acknowledging this fear, I soon felt quite happy to go on the visit.

IDEA 2: BE AFFECTED

I was going to title this "Make your partner look good", which is often used as a principle of improv. It's certainly something many people engaged in group discussions get wrong; they're so busy asserting their own views that they trample all over the comments of others.

And I'm very much in favor of making your partner look good. If you watch people doing the drawing activity, you'll notice that to begin with quite a bit of effort goes into making faces or in other ways suggesting that you've no idea what the other guy has drawn. What you'll also notice as the activity picks up is that this stuff tends to diminish. And one of the effects is that the participants each make their partner look good.

So many arguments in business get waylaid by ego, and I guess most of us struggle with whether it's our own or the other guy's.

Of course, you may be thinking this is potentially an instruction to try empty flattery. And that's why, in the end, I've opted to call this principle "Be affected".

Being affected means more than just listening to the other person and nodding. It means being willing to let what they say sink in, allowing it to influence the way you feel and respond. It's different from what often happens in conversations, where we're impatiently waiting for the other person to finish so that we can quickly lob back our already-prepared conversation grenade—a state some call "talking or reloading."

But enough theory, it's time for another activity. This one is called One Word Story, and can be played in teams of two or more.

One Word Story

What you're going to do is tell a story together, but in a slightly unusual way. If there are several of you, it will help to sit or stand in a circle.

You're going to tell it one word at a time. So the first person will say a word, then he next person will add one, and so on.

You don't need to think of a title for it and you certainly shouldn't have a planning meeting of any kind. Just let one person start with a word and go from there.

You might get lucky and find you immediately start creating coherent sentences. Or you may end up with some strange non-sequiturs. Either way, don't waste time in postmortems of any kind, or in trying to correct what others say or inviting them to say something "better." Just keep going.

Very often you'll find that amid some strange stuff, some clear sentences start to emerge. After playing for a while, pause and review your experience.

Take a moment and reflect on what you noticed.

What bits of the exercise were satisfying?

What approaches did you feel contributed to making the exercise work for you?

What do you think made it work less well?

These questions have no perfect answers, but after playing this a lot of times what emerges clearly is that in this activity making plans is a waste of time.

Many people doing this exercise have ideas about where they want the story to go and try to use their single word to drive it in a certain direction. Some are so attached to their plan that they sometimes repeat that word when their turn comes again, regardless of what others have said. Or they start planning their contribution two or more words before the one offered to them by the person right next to them.

All this is quite normal—and quite unhelpful, because it's a way of blocking out what is actually happening with your fellow participants in favor of a private scheme of your own. It's a simple way of not being affected by others.

Another thing that tends to happen is a lot of agonizing over "mistakes"—either one's own or someone else's. That's another way of holding up the flow and preventing forward movement.

If you review your experience and play again, not trying to make plans and really listening to your fellow participants, you'll likely find it a more satisfying experience. And you may be surprised at the stories that emerge—which, like the drawing in the first exercise, will be influenced by all and controlled by none.

Incidentally, in early rounds of the exercise, some players may seem to be deliberately sabotaging the round, or simply not getting it. I often find, though, when asked to reflect on how they play, these people will admit they've been trying to control the story and decide not to do it the next time. Another great thing about improv work is that people often learn the ideas for themselves, without having to be instructed.

So this is a very simple instance of what happens when we allow people to affect us, instead of trying to affect them. Of course, in longer improv exercises we develop this idea in more detail. For instance, when I'm training in customer service, I get people to think a lot more about how they empathize with complaining customers so they can develop an authentic and constructive response. It's an easy trap to just panic and rush about taking action without really understanding where the customer is coming from.

Emergence And Complexity

Think about this: in real life, organizations, brands, and ideas all emerge in the same way that this story does. They are the end product of a series of interactions over which no one player has that much control. It's fine to set a goal; in this exercise we made the goal "a story," and you can play variations where you set a title or theme or perhaps limit the number of rounds. In life, the goal might be a bit grander—for example, "to build a successful airline"—but the way you get there can't follow some detailed blueprint. It will always emerge out of the interplay of lots of fallible human beings.

In this game, we created a few simple bits of structure—the order of taking turns and the number of words each person can say. In your airline, the structures and rules are, of course, rather more numerous—but there will still be scope for flexibility in how people play at building an airline within those structures. Remember Mihaly Csikszentmihalyi from earlier in this chapter? I think this is what he means by creating an organization that stimulates the complexity of those who belong to it.

IDEA 3: EMBRACE SURPRISE

Improv teaches us to be willing to let go of control and allow ourselves to be surprised.

I confess, sometimes I can be the world's biggest control freak. And in lots of situations it's good to feel in control. Other times I want someone else to be in control: on the whole, I like airline pilots to be in control of the plane.

That's not what I'm talking about. I'm talking about letting go of the almost pathological desire to control how other human beings respond to one's own actions. Giving up that kind of control may be a bit scary but it can be a huge relief. In all the exercises so far, we abandon some control and find it makes for a more interesting life.

Here's how it works: When I relinquish control, I'm no longer solely responsible for the outcome. Suddenly, I work more freely, believing that you're a smart person and you'll probably deal with things I forget to include. And if you don't, I can always invite someone else to join in and do it. Yes, when I give up control, I often lose the pressure and stress that makes a job difficult.

This is not rocket science. (I just asked a rocket scientist and he agreed with me. He says his affidavit is in the mail but that might bulk the chapter up too much.) Groups of people can think smarter than one person. I think James Surowiecki's *Wisdom of Crowds* covered that quite well.

Kathy Sierra is a highly regarded writer who keeps a great blog called "Creating Passionate Users." She points out in her blog that we learn more from surprises:

> Think about the times you've done something that made intuitive or logical sense, but turned out to be so wrong. The times where you've said, "Whoa—I'll never do that again." Those are the memorable moments where you really learned something.

> This is where so many teachers (and books) go wrong. In trying to make the learning smooth, and in a well-intentioned attempt to save the learner from having to learn the hard way, they simply tell you in advance what to do and what not to do. If there's a surprise lurking, they just tell you up front and spare you the trouble.

> But they just robbed you of the chance to remember. To have that thing seared into your brain. What's worse, after they tell you how things really work, then they give you a lab exercise that simply demonstrates exactly what they told you. No surprises there.

Thanks, Kathy and good point. Improv creates surprises, which is why I think it has a lot to teach us—especially about the assumptions we so easily make about the world and how it works.

What characterizes good teams learning together is that people get surprised—by themselves and by their colleagues. Surprised by what they learn and by what they find they can create together.

When people in conflict move from attacking each other to establishing common ground, they are surprised. When a team trying to solve a problem suddenly gets a new insight, there is surprise. When we discover new skills in our colleagues, we're surprised.

Surprise is the hallmark of learning and collaboration and a sign that people's attention has been engaged and they are energized.

Ah, you may be saying, but I'm not good with surprises. Excellent, then perhaps you need a little practice?

New Choice

This is a simple activity that can be done in pairs. One person will be a story-teller, and the other will be the audience. (You should, of course, reverse roles so you both get to try both positions; each offers things to learn.)

The storyteller gets to tell a story. For the purposes of this exercise, it's probably easier if it's made up. It doesn't need to be a great tale, it could just be "Mr. Smith Goes to New York" or "Timmy the Hamster Reads War and Peace". The storyteller begins the tale and the listener . . . well, the listener listens.

Here's the twist: at any point, the listener can call out "New Choice," which means the storyteller has to back up a few words and then take the story in a new direction. With either a minor change or a big one. If the listener likes the new choice, the story rolls on. If not, the listener can keep calling "New Choice" until happy with the results.

Here's one way it might go . . .

Cyril was an old man living in Liverpool—

New Choice!

Cyril was an old man living in Manchester, who one morning woke up and put on his favorite blue shirt—

New Choice!

. . . woke up and put on his favorite pink shirt—

New Choice!

. . . woke up and put on a blazer—

New Choice!

. . . woke up and put on an air of smug satisfaction to impress his wife who was lying in bed next to him—

New Choice!

. . . impress his wife who was lying about her age to a newspaper reporter on the telephone. . . .

That's just an example. You can experiment with what it's like to have lots of cries of "New Choice" and not so many.

Your mileage may vary, but most people find this an entertaining exercise once they opt to go with the flow. The listener can influence the story. And the storyteller may decide that it's easier to let the listener decide what's satisfying and thus feel free to try lots of different ideas out.

For now, I'm offering New Choice as good practice in being surprised—and perhaps surprising yourself at what creative ideas you can come up with.

We are such creatures of habit, it's really good to remind ourselves that, moment by moment, we can if we wish make different choices and explore new possibilities. Think of any number of successful innovations, and you could trace them back to some entrepreneurial inventor who looked at the status quo and made a new choice.

The way to succeed as an airline is to charge high fares—New Choice!

The way to make money from music is to force customers to buy CDs—New Choice!

People will only buy books in shops where they can actually handle the product—New Choice!

But this isn't all about world-changing ideas. It can be about introducing new flexibility to our relationships—and recognizing that while it's tough to change the world, we do have some flexibility in how we respond to it.

Improv encourages us to embrace surprise because it does a great job rehabilitating spontaneity in groups. The exercises discourage postmortems in favor of taking what is given as a given and moving forward. We spend less time arguing (either in our heads or out loud) and more time exploring new possibilities.

This isn't about getting rid of criticism, but it is about reminding ourselves of the value of suspending it. Running critical thoughts is a very effective way of not listening to people, not really showing up in relationships. Critical thoughts take us out of the present and into often futile worries about the future or regrets about the past. In this sense, improv is based on a philosophy of action.

I've chosen some simple exercises that may seem to be about talking and making pictures. But improv is a performance art and these drills are key to real live performances full of movement and engagement.

In organizations, we often worry about absenteeism—the habit of not showing up to work on some false pretext. Charles Handy suggested the deeper problem is presenteeism—the pervasive habit of coming to work and not really paying attention, engaging, or sharing. One of the great things about improv exercises is that they give us all a reminder that it's actually fun and energizing to engage with each other. When this happens, things get done—not because of orders or in response to incentives, but from a primal human urge to get along and move.

THIS IS NOT A REHEARSAL

I hope you've enjoyed trying out these exercises. I believe that if you engage with them for long enough, you'll learn the improv principles intuitively, without my possibly labored explanations.

I invite you not to spend too much time evaluating what I've said here. Instead, see what happens if you apply these ideas in practice. Instead of predicting what will happen, put them to the test by seeing what does actually happen.

In that way, you'll be treating these exercises not as some theoretical activity but as a living experience. I use these activities to help groups become more creative, to resolve conflicts and to build stronger collaboration. They work on more than one level; they give people actual experiences of working together in a new way—which can be more useful than hours of analysis. At the same time, when people reflect on how they engage with these apparently lighthearted activities, they're often surprised by what they learn about themselves and their colleagues.

Sometimes these exercises can provide good warm-ups for meetings, but I think there is a lot more to them than that. If you pay attention, they can encourage lively discussions about how people work together, conversations that can lead to change where other, more literal, approaches fail.

Finally, in improv language, this essay is an *offer*, for you to respond to as you please. I'd be fascinated to hear what your experience is like. Feel free to *Yes, and* me—write to johnnie@johnniemoore.com.

From The Editor

I first got to know Johnnie through his writings on Kevin Roberts's *Lovemarks*. Johnnie didn't have many kind words about the book. His rants created wonderful conversations around branding. I have been a reader of his ever since. Johnnie is another author with a background that zigzags across topics from political speechwriting to consulting on facilitation and marketing. Johnnie has lived within walking distance of St. Paul's Cathedral (London) for almost twenty years now.

In His Own Words . . .

What is it about your essay topic that made you want to write this chapter in *More Space?*

"I love using improvisation as a way to work with people and I love sharing it. Plus I wanted an outlet for my frustration with the mass of business books that make up complicated rules that miss the mystery and excitement of being a living human being."

Jonas's Lessons:
Five Honest Letters From An IT Manager

by Jeremy Wright

Dear reader,

I am, for the moment, assuming that you have somehow stumbled upon these letters after my death. I am quite taken with the idea that I have passed on from this world. In fact, I hope so, since these letters present an embarrassing account of the kind of man I really am.

And again, since I am apparently in the assuming mood, I am assuming that you didn't know me. Because if you did, I'm not sure you would want to admit to that, having read the events I am about to describe.

It's not that I am a particularly evil man, nor is it that I have done anything particularly foolish. In fact, it's quite the opposite. As I sit here in my office, I realize that I haven't necessarily done anything memorable at all. In spite of having been given every opportunity to the contrary.

I sit here writing these letters in the hopes that the lessons I've learned will be spelled out between the lines, as it were, of the story I am about to tell. You will forgive me, dear reader, if at times I seem old, insolent, tattered, or confused. After all, for a man such as myself, few things are more disgusting than to seem to be that which I am.

I don't say all of this to sound pompous, even though that is exactly what I am. No, I say it in an attempt at honesty. Because honesty is why I am writing these letters. It—honesty—is a skill in which I am sorely out of practice. And one which it may take me several pages to perfect.

Having rambled sufficiently, I feel it is time to back up. To go back to the beginning, as it were. Perhaps even to introduce myself? Yes. It is definitely time to introduce myself and the other players on the stage of this performance I will call "Jonas's Lessons."

My name is Jonas Luck. Ironic, really, when I think about it. However, I won't go into why just now, as I have already rambled quite enough for this page. In my life, I have my work and my family. We'll leave my family out of this, as it really has nothing to do with my Lessons. And there I go, being pompous again: capitalizing "lessons." I fear this will continue, dear reader, so please forgive me as I, in spite of myself, am myself.

Getting back to the story: My name is Jonas Luck, and I am in charge of IT at one of the world's largest software development and consulting companies. That isn't to say that I am a particularly important individual in our organization, because I am not. I am simply in charge of IT at our headquarters—which means I make sure that the people who are supposed to make sure that everyone's tools are working are, in fact, doing what they are supposed to be doing. (IT is generally said to stand for Information Technology, but I often refer to it in my head as Ingenious Toodlings.)

I have been with this company for more than twenty years, which makes me one of the oldest men here. It is therefore with some embarrassment that I admit that I am merely in charge of making sure people don't slack off.

One of those people I watch is my "Jonas Thorn," Davis Stewart. He is to me as the Apostle Paul's "thorn in his side"—he doesn't go away, and torments me day and night.

That isn't to say that Davis is evil, or that he literally torments me (though sometimes it does indeed feel that this is his exact intention). Davis is a smart young man, for his age. He was fresh out of college when I hired him. That was a year before all of this began. Meanwhile, he hasn't lost his zeal for "fresh ideas" and "improving things," in spite of all of my attempts to introduce him to normal business life.

Davis really does try his best to be an asset to the little team we have here. He sends me weekly e-mails detailing his newest ideas or some of the exciting contacts he has made in the industry. Some of them request that he go to this conference or that, always followed by a "business case" rationalization for the frivolous request. It isn't, after all, as if he is visiting a client who is preparing to make a million-dollar order. Not that he would, of course, since he is in the IT department at our headquarters, which is just about as far removed from doing client visits as you can get.

Not that that bothers Davis. He is a persistent Thorn, you see. It doesn't matter how many times I tell him he's a freethinking lunatic or a fool; he simply smiles at me and tries again a few days later. The boy is full of energy. In fact, maybe that is what grates on me so: his boundless energy. He's like a puppy. A puppy that can write e-mails, call meetings, write business cases, and generally be good and valuable enough at what he actually does that I can never find cause to rid myself of him.

Now that I have rambled for yet another page, I should probably tell you what the point is of these letters you are holding. I should probably let you in on why I am, I earnestly hope, speaking from the grave.

I sit here on the eve of the second anniversary of Davis's hiring. It is odd that I mark the passage of time according to events in Davis's life and not my own. But no matter. On this anniversary of Davis's entering my life, I cannot help but be reflective. I feel a sense of impending doom, and perhaps it is this sense of doom that actually compels me to write what are, in effect, self-aggrandized tales of what I perceive to be the truth. My hope is that I will continue to document this time in my life and that I will emerge unscathed.

This will, again I am assuming, be a period of time in which I will learn many such Lessons. Lessons I intend to share with you in my own peculiar way. You may need to look for them; in fact, you may have already spotted at least one. My hope is that I will not need to spell them out. If I do, I feel that I will certainly have failed in this most simple of tasks: letting the story tell the truth.

Live well, dear reader,

Jonas Luck

IDEAS DON'T GROW A BUSINESS

Dear reader,

Davis came into my office today, practically breathless. He didn't knock. Again. You can be sure that I am not one of those bosses who say, "My office has an open door." Of course, the door does happen to be open. But it's only open to keep the air fresh—there's very poor circulation in this part of the building.

I am, in fact, quite taken with the idea that my office door isn't open at all, and that people should knock before entering. I like to call it common courtesy. A trait Davis seems to lack in every possible way.

Davis entered my office today with one of his "new ideas" that often make my head hurt. I can feel the pain coming on now just thinking about him wringing his hands,

The boy is full of energy. In fact, maybe that is what grates on me so: his boundless energy. He's like a puppy. A puppy that can write e-mails, call meetings, write business cases, and generally be good and valuable enough at what he actually does that I can never find cause to rid myself of him.

Davis entered my office today with one of his "new ideas" that often make my head hurt. I can feel the pain coming on now just thinking about him wringing his hands, sweating at the brow and generally fidgeting with excitement.

sweating at the brow and generally fidgeting with excitement.

Now, it's not as though Davis can't control himself. And it's not really as if he's completely wasting my time. He simply has a deep need to share every little thing with me, which, again, isn't common courtesy. Poor lad.

His idea today was something about "increased efficiency" by "leveraging economies of scale." I swear the boy comes up with these phrases just to lose me. I managed to fluff him off by telling him to send me an e-mail detailing his idea. It should give me a few hours of peace while he figures out the best way to try and convince me to listen to him.

The sad thing about Davis is that he tends to be more focused on other people's jobs than his own. You'd think he'd be spending his time dealing with internal customer issues instead of worrying about how best to do something or other that affects the whole company. That is, after all, what they pay me to do.

While I'd never say that Davis was particularly inefficient, it did surprise me when I received an e-mail from him not ten minutes after I sent him away. The bothersome part of the matter is that he hadn't sent me just any e-mail, he had sent me a rather detailed one with quotes and study findings and everything.

I could tell that this would be one of those issues that he wasn't going to drop very quickly. With most of his ideas, I can brush him off a few times until he goes away. But every once in a while he feels he has a particularly worthwhile idea that he actually believes in. Obviously I have a solution for this as well.

When I can't brush him off, the best way to make him stop his pony shucking is to call a meeting. And if I can invite other people of my level to the meeting, I may just be able to show them how important Davis is to the company, without actually showing them anything at all. I do enjoy killing two or three birds with one stone.

I set the meeting for two weeks away, in order to give Davis ample time to calm down before presenting to anyone. There is nothing worse than an uptight Davis doing a presentation. Except, perhaps, for an uptight Davis in my office.

The worst part of the whole plan was that Davis felt a need to e-mail me or come into my office on a daily basis with "status reports" and to "bounce ideas off of me." He does know how to be a bother, I'll give him that much.

After several of these, I asked him, quite pointedly in fact, if he thought he could actually do this presentation or if he'd require me to do it. Why, dear reader, you should have seen the look on his face! Pure horror it was, almost as if I'd said his idea, whatever it was, didn't have any merit. Which it doesn't.

The problem with Davis is that he doesn't realize that ideas simply don't help a business grow. A focus on doing your part of the work will do far more for any company than thinking up new ways to "innovate" and "engage."

Poor lad, I'm hoping that this time I can teach him that lesson.

Suffice it to say that the day of the presentation came and Davis did well enough—at least, when compared to his past performances. There were PowerPoint slides and animations and quotes from the Gartner Group. If I hadn't had an overly large breakfast that morning, I might have been impressed. In fact, it was going so well I thought I might have to ask a pointed question that would strip Davis of all that confidence.

Thankfully, the accounting manager beat me to it when he asked Davis if this would "actually make us any money." Davis almost missed a beat when he responded that it would save "soft dollars" by "increasing efficiency."

> The problem with Davis is that he doesn't realize that ideas simply don't help a business grow. A focus on doing your part of the work will do far more for any company than thinking up new ways to "innovate" and "engage."

I could tell that Dayne, the accounting manager, wasn't listening when his eyes glazed over completely.

I felt it was time to ask the all-important question of cost. Davis pulled up a chart that detailed how, even though his plan would cost some amount of money, the company would make it back in six months. I asked him if that was a personal guarantee, which made him visibly flinch.

Davis's problem is largely that he doesn't understand what he doesn't understand. I have no desire, nor does anyone at the company, to spend money to potentially save money. Granted, some of his past ideas have saved us money—I've allowed them because they didn't cost us anything. However, when he starts talking about "efficiencies," I can always tell he hasn't realized that a potential savings is never as good as a real one. It's completely unrealistic for him to expect Dayne, our accounting manager, to give him money simply to do whatever he feels like doing so that his idea might, one day, if everything goes well, save the company only a little bit more than the project actually ended up costing.

I had thought the meeting had served its purpose, until Davis sent me a post-meeting e-mail asking me what I thought.

I always hate open-ended questions because they require a response. Responses require me to reflect on what was said, which is difficult when I wasn't really listening. Meetings are rarely about actually communicating anything, at least in the presentations. The valuable part of attending meetings is often what people say after the meeting—only then will you get to find out what's really happening in the company.

I get the feeling that "what's really happening" is something Davis is missing. My response to him attempted to drive that home by relying on phrases like "low-hanging fruit," which I'm sure he'll enjoy. It may even raise his respect and awe of me, and that's never a bad thing.

In my experience, e-mail is where conversations go to die and meetings are where ideas go to die. My hope is that this little idea of his will simply go away.

Live well, dear reader,

Jonas Luck

Some Things Don't Go As Planned

Dear reader,

I honestly believe that in a past life I must have been a dolphin. Swimming, splashing, and playing all day somehow seems to agree with some deep part of who I am. Maybe it's that there are no consequences in a dolphin world; or maybe it's that the ocean is so big that, if something goes awry, you can always find another part of the ocean to swim, splash, or play in.

Alas, in this life I am not a dolphin—not even close. I haven't been swimming in years, I would look completely undignified doing so, and the last time I played was when my children were toddlers. No, in this life I am not a dolphin. In spite of having a day in which I wished that I could simply find another corner of the ocean to frolic in.

For you see, dear reader, today was not an ordinary day, in any sense of the word "ordinary." In fact, today was one of the worst days I've ever heard of. It started, as always, with seeing Davis. Thankfully he didn't say anything, but his mere presence was nearly enough to sour my thoughts of getting any quality work done. Maybe it was the way he was working, or maybe it was even the fact that he was working so diligently. I could just tell that yesterday's delaying tactics hadn't changed his resolve at all.

In my experience, e-mail is where conversations go to die and meetings are where ideas go to die.

As I walked past my secretary, she informed me that there was an "emergency strategic meeting." Though I'm not entirely sure what that means, hearing "emergency" and "strategic" in the same sentence is nearly as daunting as hearing "emergency" and "meeting" in the same sentence. Believe you me, dear reader, hearing all three words jumbled together in such a haphazard fashion did nothing to improve my mood.

Thankfully, the meeting had already started, so I was saved from any initial opening salvo of issues. Hopefully everyone involved had settled in, started drinking their coffee, and started tuning out.

I made my way to the meeting after picking up my "executive briefcase" and was surprised to find that the room was packed. There must have been thirty people inside, and not one of them was a low-ranking assistant. There were, quite literally, people from all across the company and around the world at this little meeting.

I found it interesting that I only heard about the meeting this morning, when obviously others must have heard about it days before. No matter, I thought to myself, as I found a chair at the back of the room and settled in for what might just be an entertaining show.

Before I heard what the presenter was saying, I noticed that it was the Chief Financial Officer (I'll refer to him as the CFO from now on) who was up there. This was the first time I'd seen Teddy in more than five years, as he was always off traveling and "making the deal" or some such nonsense. I always found it odd that one of the most important people in the company spent no more than ten days a year at the company headquarters.

I finally tuned in to the fact that Teddy was talking, and in a rather grave manner at that. He was saying something about "focus on the bottom line" and "inefficiencies across the company" and "drastic measures." I do believe that is when my ears perked up. "Drastic measures" is almost as dire as "emergency strategic meeting." Thankfully, I thought, there were no "immediate drastic measures."

Sadly, dear reader, the next words out of Teddy's mouth were "truly immediate drastic measures." My day was ruined. There wasn't a thing to be done about it. I coughed softly enough for a few heads to turn, which caused Teddy to pause and look directly at me.

I asked him what all of this actually meant. He seemed taken aback by my directness. I assure you, dear reader, that he was no more taken aback than I was when he said "truly immediate drastic measures." The man deserved a taste of his own medicine, I tell you!

I will save you the details of the rest of the four-hour meeting, because there are far too many painful moments to recall. The long and short of the "truly immediate drastic measures" was that every department needed to account for every staff member, every project, and every dollar spent over the last five years. It seems that the company was on the verge of collapse—hence these "drastic measures."

One would think an internal audit would have sufficed; something I am quite skilled at, I might add. Apparently, an internal audit wasn't what was in the cards. What was in the cards were the heads of every senior manager across the company. Any departments that didn't fall into line, and any manager which could not make a proper accounting of himself, would immediately (and, I imagine, "truly") be axed.

It was, I can tell you, rather unnerving to see thirty of my colleagues all adjusting their neckties as if to ensure their craniums were still attached.

Thankfully, I had consumed and enjoyed the good breakfast my wife served this morning, so I had my wits about me. I noted to Teddy that my department had several innovative new ideas that we felt could make a significant difference, if given a chance. Teddy nearly jumped over the table at me, and, I'm sure, nearly planted a "true and immediate" kiss on my left cheek. After the meeting, he asked me for details and I told him, without really thinking, about Davis and his many thoughts to save the company. Teddy told me I could have whatever resources I required, within reason.

I assume he means within my reason, not within Davis's, as I know that Davis would happily eat up every dollar in the company to fulfill his flights of fancy.

I, however, must get used to this. I have effectively pinned, in my foolish zeal to save my own neck, the entire department on Davis and his "ingenuity." A large part of me can't wait to tell him that I will be green-lighting some of his projects. I will need to be careful, you see, that Davis doesn't get bigheaded, and that none of the credit goes directly to him.

My hope, dear reader, is that I can distract Teddy for long enough to ensure that "OK" is good enough. I would, after all, hate to do some of these "innovative" ideas only to have them fail and have us be in a worse condition than if I'd simply kept my mouth shut.

But I assure you that I will not let us fail. My years of experience and my ability to calm a situation will surely come in handy over the next few months as I endeavor to save not only my department but, more important, my parking space.

Live well, dear reader,

Jonas Luck

Looking Ahead Through A Rearview Mirror

Dear reader,

As I am sure you are aware, there are times when life crawls along slower than a snail going uphill in January in Alaska, and there are times where you feel more like a long-lost Andretti brother than a normal human being. I can tell you honestly, dear reader, that until recently I had felt entirely like that poor frozen snail.

After my last letter to you, many things changed around here. And they changed in such a way that I was propelled to learn to go faster and further than I had done in many, many years.

In fact, the last few months have been a completely new experience for me in many ways. Several of my peers were released from their duties, several departments were merged, and the overall mood of the entire company changed nearly overnight. Every-where, that is, except for my little corner of the world.

That isn't to say that things are going incredibly well here, but somehow we've been safe from what is happening outside; principally because of how busy we have been. I have given Davis more free rein than I'd ever imagined possible, and it has certainly been entertaining to watch.

He immediately went about renegotiating with our computer and network suppliers, and worked out a leasing deal that saved us millions of dollars on paper. Sadly, several users lost files and such when the new machines came in, and we ended up having to purchase an extended support agreement that nearly wiped out any savings. However, the move looked very, very good to Teddy, our CFO. It's almost as if seeing us do something was more important than having us account for doing nearly nothing over the last several years.

Now, I can't say I approve of all of Davis's ideas. No, many of them are still entirely foolish. Just last week he proposed installing a wireless network, which he claimed would save lots of "soft dollars" because people would be able to get laptops and work from anywhere, including meetings. The thought of having people on the lawn out front working was appealing, but I knew that this was just another one of his old schemes. I'd heard it before, and I wasn't being sucked in purely on account of his zeal.

Then there was the new storage solution Davis brought in. The project went over budget, didn't meet our expectations, and is generally no better than our previous solution. Teddy didn't seem to mind, but I nearly fired Davis for not thinking the whole thing through.

All in all, dear reader, it has been an exciting time. I have managed to earn an increasing amount of kudos and, with it, a parking spot right in front of the building—though I suspect this could be because half of the senior managers have been quietly let go. No matter. There are perks to every dark cloud, and the ability to park my car within walking distance of my office is certainly one I am not going to pass up. Nor let go of easily.

Sadly, on the organizational front, the changes that were made didn't make much of a difference. There were lots of meetings, and even more e-mail, about how things needed to change. I would have pointed out my philosophy on meetings and e-mails to Teddy but that would have required, ironically, either a meeting or an e-mail to explain.

Yes, it has been an exciting time. But excitement also carries its challenges. Davis is obviously bolder than he's ever been before. I think he honestly believes it has become his duty to come up with ideas. I fear that I haven't been tempering his expectations nearly enough. It could be because I've begun actually answering his e-mail, inviting him to other meetings, and so forth. He may have become something of an icon in the company, which is a bit odd considering how little of the credit has gone directly to him.

For instance, yesterday he came in and invited me to a meeting that he was calling with other "key people in the organization." I was taken aback; not only by the fact that he had started calling meetings but also by the reality that none of the people in the room were actually all that important to the company. None even supervised a single individual.

It seemed to me as if the entire meeting was all about generating new ideas. There was even a certain level of animosity in the air toward me, which was odd as I barely even knew these people. My suspicion is that this was actually Davis calling a meeting purely to show me how much power he had, and that he was able to sway people's opinions. I was able to change that rather quickly though.

You see, dear reader, while the last few months have been rather new and rather exciting, I haven't forgotten my all-important ability to stall a meeting or conversation completely. All it really took were a few "how will this affect the bottom line?" questions and a few rolls of the eyes when I was told by each individual that this was a "soft dollar" savings that "increased efficiency" for me to realize that Davis had simply found a group of like-minded digital hippies.

They obviously didn't understand the trouble the company was in, or they wouldn't be worried about these "soft dollars." What we needed was to save real money, not this soft stuff. The company needed a leader capable of keeping free thinkers like this under control. Obviously this wasn't the first time these hippies had met; and, equally obviously, they had been left to their own devices for far too long.

I immediately realized that I'd been let into the inner sanctum of a group that consid-

I fear that I haven't been tempering his expectations nearly enough. It could be because I've begun actually answering his e-mail, inviting him to other meetings, and so forth. He may have become something of an icon in the company, which is a bit odd considering how little of the credit has gone directly to him.

ered themselves noble, intelligent, and important. While I could easily shut the group down by letting their managers know that they were doing activities other than their duties on company time, I thought it might be useful to play along. And let me tell you, dear reader, that I was a master actor in playing along.

I started to listen to their ideas, I asked for detailed reports and other kinds of minor activities designed to keep them spinning their wheels. I had, in one fell swoop, assembled a "task force" that would quickly propel me to even greater heights. They even came up with a little name for themselves, once they realized that I was "behind" them: Task Force 42. I'm not sure why they wouldn't be "Jonas's Task Force." But no matter.

Now not only was my department busy but I had just acquired even more staff from other departments that I could keep busy as well. If Teddy didn't think I was indispensable before, he would find out very quickly just how hard to replace I could be.

My intent isn't to run these poor kids into the ground but to ensure that they are kept busy with reports, surveys, meetings with vendors, and weekly Task Force 42 status reports, which I, ironically, have e-mailed to me. Some weeks I even read them.

Yes, my last letter detailed one of the worst days of my life; but this is certainly turning out to be a bumper year. More power, more authority, a larger team, and a better parking spot. Yes, dear reader, I have surely arrived.

Live well, dear reader,

Jonas Luck

The Future Can Be Shocking

Dear reader,

They say that in the heat of passion you lose all perception of time, what people think of you, and where things are going. In the last few months I have experienced just that: a complete lack of perception.

Things were going well on the various projects Davis was doing. Looking back, many of them actually made perfect sense: this is, perhaps, the problem. We consolidated servers, re-tendered all of our maintenance deals, reevaluated many of our fixed-cost services (such as Web connectivity), and released several new tools to our user base to help them be more effective.

I believe that the organization is better for it. I can't say we necessarily saved any money, though. Which was supposed to be the point. But, then, looking back on my earlier letters I realize that I was never looking to save money; so, I guess in that aspect, I have succeeded brilliantly.

I suppose I should tell you before we go any further that I am no longer with my employer. I was offered a generous early departure package and decided to take it. Part of the reason I accepted is that it was a nice package and, even though I live to work, I wouldn't mind a holiday. The real reason, though, is that Davis had become the de facto manager anyway. He was calling meetings, thinking up ideas, and basically calling all the shots. It was my job to simply say no when his ideas were foolish enough. And, I must admit, that was happening less and less frequently in recent months.

It seems that I may have overstepped my bounds. I may have worked myself out of a job, which isn't a feeling I am used to.

My gut tells me that now is the time to look back and see what I have learned. While this wasn't the original point of these letters, it seems to be a salient enough one, given what's recently happened.

> I suppose I should tell you before we go any further that I am no longer with my employer.

I can't promise, dear reader, that I will be as objective an observer as I have previously been. I am, after all, still in a fair amount of shock as a result of not having to go to work every morning. I do still get up at 4 A.M., shower and get dressed, shave, and organize my briefcase. Some mornings, I nearly get out to the car before I realize that I could have simply slept in.

Perhaps it is the ultimate irony that, now that I am able to sleep in, I have no desire to do so. Which is why I sit here now, writing this letter. I have been awake for four hours, and the rest of the house is still as quiet as can be. I am left to my thoughts more than is comfortable these days, and many of the thoughts are foreign to me.

I wonder, for instance, if Davis really has the potential to run my department. I wonder how he'd fare at higher-level meetings where his ideas would be shot down and the games of power would play out—while he, most likely, remained completely oblivious to them. I wonder if maybe he can change that, just as he somehow managed to change my department, and even, in some way, me.

In my wonderings, there comes an unbidden thought: if Davis had this potential all along, why did I get in his way?

You must understand, dear reader, that this is not how I typically think. Even questioning this thought isn't how I typically think. Which leads me to believe that something has quite obviously changed. Something profound.

As I look back over the last few years of change in the organization, I can't help but wonder if I could have done more good. I've never really strived to do "good" before; at least, not at work. After all, companies are in it for themselves, so why shouldn't their employees be in it for themselves as well?

And, as I look back, several things are clear to me. Others are hazy and indistinct, but they seem to be just as important as the ideas that are clear, if not more so.

I realize now, quite clearly, that conversation is more important than power. I realize that I could have sat down and actually talked to Davis about what kind of man he was anytime during the last several years. Perhaps it was merely a product of Davis being in the kind of environment he was in.

The fact that I took advantage of the faults of human nature by encouraging Davis to communicate via e-mail, where I am still convinced information goes to die, is perhaps evidence of my inability to actually be human in front of anyone at work.

Perhaps these letters will be the only fragment of humanity to ever make its way into the visible world. Perhaps you, dear reader, will be the only person ever to know this side of me.

I regret now that I lived a life of mediocrity. I regret that I only did things well enough to not get personal glory, and that I never encouraged Davis to shine. Regret is such a new thing to me, though. I also envy Davis for having the time to make a difference. I am gone now, but he may well be there for years to come—making a difference every day he stays.

It seems that so much of what happened at the organization was a waste of time, a waste of resources, and a waste of thought. I know it wasn't just me that tried to slow things down, as many of us often laughed about the things the "young pups" were trying to do. I know now that those young pups were the inevitable result of our lack of ability to actually *do* anything. While we loved to stall, they loved to do.

My fear now is that I will be condemned to a desire to *do*, to make a difference, in spite of having no outlet in which to *do* at all. Sure, I could garden, or take up golf. But somehow that seems just as worthwhile as using e-mail and meetings to stop com-

In my wonderings, there comes an unbidden thought: if Davis had this potential all along, why did I get in his way?

munication, or starting projects simply to try and save money (or my job).

I suppose I shouldn't complain. I was never one to believe in karma, dear reader, but it seems it doesn't matter. It seems karma believes in me. As I said before, these days I have a lot of time to devote to thought. I can't promise anything worthwhile will come out of that time. But, perhaps, these letters will prove that I wasn't completely idle, nor was I completely useless, in the years after I learned to live.

Live well, dear reader,

Jonas Luck

YEARS LATER

But he also remembered that it was thanks to Jonas that he was the man he was today.

Davis quietly put down the letters and leaned back. The labor of the process weighed heavily on his mind. He had read, and reread, these letters until the words were burned into his mind.

At first, he didn't know why Jonas's widow insisted that he accept the packet of letters. He wasn't even aware Jonas had died until she called. He had never met Mrs. Luck. And, when he did, it was only for the briefest of moments as she handed the letters to him. She told him she didn't feel it right to keep them, since they were obviously intended for him.

As Davis read through the first letters, he lacked any comprehension as to why the letters would be for him. He remembered the bitterness he'd felt toward Jonas. He remembered Jonas's inability to see past his desk, and his lack of desire to effect change in the organization.

But he also remembered that it was thanks to Jonas that he was the man he was today.

It had been many years since Jonas had left the company. Not so many that Davis forgot him, but enough that the old ways of doing things had largely been left behind. Davis often asked himself how Jonas would feel about the new company, with its forward-thinking, customer-centric focus. He wondered if Jonas would appreciate that Davis gave each of his employees the time and place they needed to voice new ideas.

He was sure that Jonas would merely lean back, arch his fingers together, and smile in that absurdly knowing way that meant he wasn't even listening to you. Davis had gotten to know that look many times. He had even appropriated it. He called it his "poker face."

After all, every CEO needs to hide his true feelings sometimes, even Davis Stewart.

FROM THE EDITOR

Jeremy's blog:
www.ensight.org

Jeremy's favorite blogs:
www.problogger.net
www.darrenbarefoot.com
www.joystiq.com

Recommended reading:
www.slackermanager.com

If you spend any time reading blogs, it is hard to miss Jeremy. Things got exciting last year when he auctioned his own skills in blog consulting on eBay. His auction was the most viewed one of the month and it got picked up by the CBS Marketwatch website. A month later, he was fired from his day job for blogging about that company's equipment and the lack of work being assigned to him. He now does all sorts of writing including an upcoming book of his own called *Blog Marketing* (due to be released at the end of 2005). He also runs insideblogging.com, a consulting company that helps businesses establish blogs. And he does all this within view of the Bay of Fundy (New Brunswick, Canada).

In His Own Words . . .

What is it about your essay topic that made you want to write this chapter in *More Space*?

"Having been in information technology, business, and management for ten years, I know most of us have many habits that if we could only break them would make us much more effective at our jobs. Originally I'd written this as "Five Things to Fix in IT," but it seemed so dry. Instead, I've illustrated these five things with a narrative—one where we can see ourselves in all the characters and their flaws. While it may not be as to-the-point as my original plan, my hope is that it will stick in readers' heads much more than it would have otherwise."

Marketing: What's Love Got to Do With It?

by Evelyn Rodriguez

Society needs a return to spiritual values—not to offset the material but to make it fully productive. . . . Mankind needs the return to spiritual values, for it needs compassion. It needs the deep experience that the Thou and the I are one, which all higher religions share.

—Peter Drucker

I confess—for most of my life, I was the quintessential "functionally guarded" person.

I mean that in the Alcoholics Anonymous sense: someone who manages remarkably well in the public eye while spending great swatches of time under the influence is "functionally alcoholic." As long as you don't get too close or peek behind the curtain, all is well in Oz.

I'm also a recovering computer engineer. The day I stepped into marketing (even though it was technical marketing), my fellow geeks viewed my shift as "going over to the dark side." Their wrinkled noses revealed their distaste for the subjectivity and nuances; anything involving interpersonal communication was "politics," as far as they were concerned.

I tended to agree. Hiding in numbers, code, concrete forms, and the formulaic is a safe place for the functionally guarded. I could avoid the self-conscious discomfort I had with emotion, with softness and the vulnerability potentially exposed by dabbling in the realm of people. In his new book *A Whole New Mind,* Dan Pink insightfully points out that the reclaiming of the "right brain" follows the path of the archetypal hero's journey. But Pink never addresses the central fear of embarking on this journey: the seeming descent into hell. While I might be worried that my job will be shipped to Bangalore, I'm even more terrified of going into the abyss of my right mind. Left-brainers may avoid expressing feelings—but they definitely have them.

A lot has happened since I entered marketing. But first and foremost, I've come to the conclusion that the "functionally guarded" stance just isn't functional any longer. And not just for me. I don't know if you are feeling the pain yet, but if you are paying attention, something must seem amiss in global media and markets today.

The media are a harbinger of things to come. As Marshall McLuhan pointed out, the act of creating, viewing, participating, or engaging in media alters the human nervous system. Media literally mess with your mind. Deeply ingrained patterns of thought reinforced by biochemistry can be loosened and new brain terrain explored after the emergence of a new medium.

If the media serve as a leading indicator—a canary in the coal mine, so to speak—then what are blogs and other participatory media signaling? Or perhaps it's a chicken-and-egg phenomenon? Do new media structures arise after individual and collective mind-sets and thus worldviews emerge?

No matter. The point is that for the first time ever, we now see at least three worldviews, or decision-making frameworks, clashing in the media. And even more in the marketplace. The working assumption that everyone holds the same frame of reference used to work just fine—when a single predominant worldview governed business and media.

We may never fully understand each other at a conceptual level of discourse. I've spoken with corporate executives who were sincerely perplexed when ordinary people they run into at the local Whole Foods—that is, non-anarchists—swarmed into Seattle to protest at the World Trade Organization meeting. On the other extreme, friends who tried to talk me into going to a teach-in at those protests couldn't grasp how or why I could see any merit in the other side of the globalization debate.

For strategists, innovators, and marketers, the challenge is that developing and marketing an innovative product that meets deep-seated and even unstated needs requires more than reading people, more than understanding people; it requires knowing others as ourselves. Paradoxically, this knowing does not mean voting for the same candidate, going to the same church, buying the same SUV, watching the same reality TV shows, coming from the same corner of the world, or even having the same motivation for waking up each morning. You can still relate to others (and market to them) when you don't entirely grasp their worldview.

Everything Happened After 1996

New forms of media don't emerge whole from a hermit's cave. Media are deeply informed by current times. Likewise, the times deeply inform media. And these are interesting times indeed if we look at the last ten years against the backdrop of history. Business and media are relatively new institutions, historically speaking, and they've both spent most of their existence in equilibrium—with everyone involved holding more or less the same worldview. That is, until now.

I believe that we are successful when our ways are suited to the times and circumstances, and unsuccessful when they are not. For one sees that, in the things that lead to the end which everyone aims at, that is, glory and riches, men proceed in different ways.

—Niccolo Machiavelli

Machiavelli's work—written in 1513—is still commonly cited in business schools as support for the claim that we, Homo sapiens, are driven by self-interest.

In *Non-Zero: The Logic of Human Destiny*, Richard Wright sets out to map self-interest over the "arrow of the history of life, from the primordial ooze to the World Wide Web." Moving from cave survival to tribal clans to feudal empires to church states to nation states to corporate states and onward, we've become increasingly interdependent, Wright says.

Wright isn't chanting a Woodstockian chorus of harmony and world peace. It's not a matter of altruism as he sees it—we've simply become so intertwined and interdependent in our social structures that my self-interest is enveloped and enmeshed with your self-interest. In terms of game theory, it's a "non-zero game," which comes down to this: we all win or we all lose.

The thing that sticks in my mind about *Non-Zero* is the way the theme of expanding cooperative self-interest captured the imagination of attendees at the first Accelerating Change conference a few years back. This is an audience of ardent futurists, uber-geeks, and a few financiers of the future. On the surface the audience appears to be a Darwinian-Machiavellian brew where the fittest cyborg triumphs. But following Richard Wright's keynote, the conference bookstore sold out of his book within minutes.

Machiavelli is worth repeating: "We are successful when our ways are suited to the times and circumstances, and unsuccessful when they are not." Over the course of history we've steadily moved from an egocentric to an ethnocentric to an increasingly world-centric perspective. Our minds cannot help but be informed and influenced by the worldviews of our culture and our times.

And our times have changed, so we need new thought patterns. *New times, new thinking*. That's the catchphrase of *Spiral Dynamics* (by Don Beck and Christopher Cowan), a book that outlines the evolution of human concepts—including the leading indicators to societal shifts in thought patterns—throughout history, capturing what's happening now right before it started.

Think about 1996—the year that *Spiral Dynamics* came out. Beck and Cowan probably submitted their final manuscript before Netscape went public on August 9, 1995. And certainly before the November 1995 launch of *Fast Company*. And the blogosphere wasn't even a gleam in anyone's eye yet. San Francisco had cheap rents south of Market Street and my mom hadn't heard of Sand Hill Road. The twin towers were intact and the media were the bailiwick of hip New Yorkers and not scraggly "citizen journalists." I hadn't joined the Internet revolution, er, I mean industry as yet—unless you count being addicted to online communities. Nor had I yet been married . . . or divorced. Ah, 1996. That's the same year that Cindy Olsen joined Enron as VP of corporate affairs in charge of the 401(K) program—oh so many eons before she would "diversify" her own personal holdings and withdraw her millions. Geez, perhaps everything did happen after 1996.

Seeing Through The Kaleidoscope

Before I get carried away harking back to 1996, a few concepts need definition and fleshing out.

For starters, you'll need to know what a meme is. Richard Dawkins introduced the term into our lexicon in *The Selfish Gene*. Since then it and its implications have spread like, well, like a meme is wont to do, like wildfire. A meme is defined as the basic unit of cultural transmission, or imitation. It can be just about any contagious and attractive idea or concept.

A value-meme (to use a term coined by Beck and Cowen, whose work is based on research by psychologist Clare Graves) is a coherent set of beliefs and concepts that compose and inform your decision-making framework. In a sense, the value-meme isn't any single meme but an entire container of memes that gathers additional reinforcing and aligning memes. It helps me to picture the value-meme as something akin to what complexity theory calls a strange attractor—more or less drawing in matching memes and repelling others—or simply as a bucket o'memes. The value-meme helps explain why "red" states and "blue" states don't always see eye to eye whether it's pre- or post-Election 2004, why the best-selling *The Purpose-Driven Life* with its universal themes is restricted to a market of traditional churchgoers, why the "cause marketing" of ecologically minded businesses like The Body Shop attracts a cultlike following, and why environmentalists and cattle ranchers don't chat together at the local diner.

New value-memes don't just come out of the blue. Like any trend they start as a gurgling trickle before joining the river of cultural norms. I'm sure there were a few folks who thought I was eerily prescient when I lived in Utah. I'd be the one asking oddball questions about applying software engineering methodologies to globally distributed teams as scattered as the Philippines, India, and Bulgaria. They hadn't begun to insist that offshoring was an anomaly and not a significant happening—it wasn't even on the radar screen. Yet. But my forecasts are not magical. Spend enough time traveling to the East and West Coast—and to Silicon Valley if you are tech forecasting—and it doesn't take a rocket scientist or a psychic to see particular trends that have taken hold on the coasts eventually heading toward the middle states. Nope, not magic. But it does take a willingness to be a dispassionate observer, withholding judgment from either extreme: denial and resistance on one side and enthusiastically jumping on every bandwagon on the other.

■ **Blue:** The blue value-meme prizes civic and religious institutions. Law, order, and stability come through rules and regulations, and all events proceed according to a divine plan. People are saints or sinners. It is the basis for nation states.

■ **Orange:** Derived from the modernism of the Enlightenment, the orange value-meme prizes rationality and objective truth, emphasizes individual achievement, and divides people between winners and losers. It is the basis for corporate states.

■ **Green:** The green value-meme differentiates systems and applies values that are relative and pluralistic. The idea is not to marginalize anyone; it is egalitarian and consensus-based, and often views hierarchies as oppressive. Its goal is to liberate people from greed and dogma and establish linked communities, and it divides people between oppressed and oppressors. It is the basis for "value communities."

■ **Yellow:** The yellow value-meme integrates systems and explores open systems and networked meshes. It reintroduces vertical hierarchies and ranking, grasps big pictures, and tends to be expressive rather than impressive. Rather than creating a duality of any sort, it tends to accept people and values—while not necessarily agreeing with their varying worldviews. It is the basis for "integral commons."

In the same vein, perhaps it's no surprise that organic foods purveyor Whole Foods is growing wildly, spiritual and New Age titles are underground bestsellers, *Worthwhile* and *Breathe* magazines both launched within the last few months, green and sustainable catchwords in business are multiplying, grassroots marketing is prevalent, *The Cluetrain Manifesto* is the bible of the blogosphere, and "corporate social responsibility" has crept its way into annual reports. The seeds were planted by the Baby Boomers as far back as the 1960s. So the anti-establishment fervor of the documentary *The Corporation*, the book *No Logo,* and the WTO protests are all quite nostalgic.

But the world was not ready for the sixties in the 1960s. That was a time and place more suited to the emergence of the yuppie than the hippie. Yet there was no denying that a scattering of people on the lunatic fringe didn't quite look at the world like everyone else, and were not motivated or concerned with quite the same things as the rest of us.

In the 1940s Abraham Maslow conducted hundreds of interviews, discovering that people—and even the very same person at different stages of life—don't always have the same driving and motivating forces behind why they do what they do. And thus his famous hierarchy of needs pyramid made news. Then in the 1960s and 1970s Clare W. Graves also conducted interview after interview—and noticed a new pattern of thought emerging in individual mind-sets. He codified this pattern, assigning letters to designate individual and societal motivators in a nested hierarchy, a scheme Beck and Cowan later described in terms of a palette of colors that serve as mnemonics for the codes.

Because of its roots in the Graves letter-codes, this color palette doesn't quite follow the visible spectrum; it starts with beige, then runs through purple, red, blue, orange, green, yellow, turquoise, coral, and other colors that don't come up often enough to discuss here. It's easiest to think of it as a set of nested Russian dolls: with the tiny beige doll nestled in the very center, fully enclosed by a slightly larger purple doll, and so on. And it is notable that yellow marks a distinctive and dramatic shift to a new "second tier" level, making a break from preceding colors—it reflects an expansive view relatively free from fear and self-protection. People who read Graves's or Beck and Cowen's work often jump to the conclusion that these colors represent archetypes—basically types of people. For instance, I'm blue, you're yellow, and she's green. Incorrect assumption. While individuals may hold a dominant orientation, the colors represent adaptive perspectives within people—what I think of as worldviews, or value-memes. Also, someone could definitely exhibit an orange streak in business while leaning toward blue value-memes in other interactions.

In the left margin is an ultra-brief summary of the four predominant worldviews in industrialized nations today.

This dizzying rainbow serves to stress the way our society now includes a multitude of conflicting worldviews that did not have critical mass only a decade ago. We can no longer assume that others hold our own worldview. Nonetheless, it really is possible to relate to others outside your own worldview without mentally juggling a table of colors in your daily business interactions—a point I return to later in this chapter.

But first, the promised flashback to 1996. That long stable period between the Enlightenment and the Internet isn't as monochromatic orange as I'm about to make it, of course. Nor has the business world made the crossover from orange to green. However, we are for the first time living on a world stage where orange, green, and now yellow are all players.

The Revolution Will Not Be Televised

Here's What We've Set Out To Do: Identify the values of the revolution and the people who are building companies that embody them: a commitment to merge economic growth with social justice, democratic participation with tough-minded execution, explosive technological innovation with old-fashioned individual commitment.

—Handbook of the Business Revolution: Manifesto, *Fast Company*, November 1995 (premiere issue)

I'm doing an (free) operating system (just a hobby, won't be big and professional like gnu) for 386(486) AT clones.

—Linus Torvalds, 1991, describing the launch of Linux

Enter Orange Stage Left

The Industrial Age ushered in the rise of the corporation and the values of the American Dream: achievement, status, prestige, and the tangible rewards of working hard and prospering by toil and ingenuity.

Branding became imperative after the surpluses that followed World War II. And it was cemented as a marketing vehicle in the June Cleaver era of the 1950s when everyone scurried to watch the very same television shows—back when mass media really did attract mass audiences.

Mostly business as we knew it throughout the twentieth century brought no abrupt upheavals—until a big wrench was thrown among the factory cogs. And that wrench was a new medium called the Internet.

Enter Green Stage Right

The Internet marked the first time we all had access to a global warehouse of information at our fingertips. We could now connect to practically any other person in the world. From its origins in sharing information and research within universities and scientific labs, the 'Net became recognized as a distribution platform where anyone with a business plan on a napkin could turn a buck. Frictionless commerce! Disintermediation! The prophets of the New Economy extolled the glories of the new medium. Fragmented marketplaces coalesced easily at sites like eBay and craigslist.

The fabric of the World Wide Web is made up of hyperlinks—the lateral linking structure that connects one document to another. Suddenly it was no longer necessary to create every last line of content—instead, you could simply reuse, reference, and link to other documents, including those you didn't own yourself. If it was out there in the ether, or in "the cloud," to use an industry insider name for the Internet, anyone could connect to it. The act of clicking on a site and following links to other pages and sites even on its own yielded far more interactivity and user control than sitting on the couch watching TV or sipping coffee and skimming the morning paper ever did. And interactivity could go well beyond merely surfing. Passionate users of online communities such as The Well, Prodigy, CompuServe, and AOL catalyzed the explosive growth of Internet communities in all their variations—forums, discussion groups, and e-mail lists. For any community of interest—no matter how esoteric, eccentric, or absurd—you could easily find and communicate with kindred spirits and like-minded folks who shared your passion.

The decentralized, distributed nature of the massively global network eventually alters the way you look at solving nearly any complex problem. I noted this for myself and for the visionaries, engineers, and financiers around me. From Napster's massive decentralized architecture to *Small Pieces, Loosely Joined* to *The Wisdom of Crowds,* complex adaptive systems thinking both intrigued and threatened holders of existing value-memes.

The competitive pace of the New Economy meant that creative destruction was now wired and equilibrium was tired—even in old lumbering behemoths. The Silicon Valley culture of "ideas trump titles" spread worldwide. Top down procedures and bureaucratic processes were scrapped like hourglasses in an era running on Internet time. The catchphrase "24/7" entered our vocabulary. *Fail early, fail often.* Business plans morphed faster than software could be cranked out. Cowboy coding: Whip it out and lasso it together pronto. A scalable Web site meant it wouldn't be obsolete and architecturally brittle before the next trade show or venture capital pitch.

Allegiance wasn't to your company but to your guild—or, ahem, to the start up with the biggest foozball table, the best on-site masseuse, and the sportiest car thrown in as a signing bonus. Work was supposed to be fun and fast. Staid and rigid hierarchies were the last place freshly minted MBAs were headed. The spoils were to be shared too, and more egalitarian stock options made sure that employment carried an aura of ownership.

Personally, I was enthralled by the fast paced ride recounted in *eBoys: The First Inside Account of Venture Capital at Work* and sincerely gripped by business plan writing and IPO prospectus reading.

By late 1999 I was just plain crazed; I accepted a position as CTO of a brand-new VC backed start up while continuing full-time work for the next three months to make sure my stock options vested. I had no time for the mountain wedding my fiancé and I had wanted, so we ducked over to the courthouse. I really didn't have time for marriage (or people for that matter, either).

The New Economy wasn't just about calculating how many millions our stock options would be worth when we IPO'd and photocopying and distributing *Fast Company* articles. And then again it was about calculating how many millions my stock options would be worth. I could always do what I really meant to do . . . someday.

But things aren't ever as cut-and-dried as they appear. While the year 2000 marked the peak of my "orange" period, at the exact same time I considered Rachel Carson my hero, belonged to Greenpeace, ran a regional "progressive" women's e-zine as a side venture, and led a biweekly breakfast "business and consciousness" roundtable. At the roundtable we'd chat about the thoughts of Peter Senge, Dee Hock, Margaret Wheatley, and Anita Roddick.

The infamous RIAA versus Napster case was the classic portrayal of two worlds, or two value-memes, colliding. Pitted mano a mano was: "we can win this game only if we own the content" against "let's share and we'll see what innovations and business models emerge down the road."

It was a toxic concoction: one part "change-the-world" and one part "fuck the establishment," with one part "yeah, a condo in Vail would be sweet" and a dash of hubris thrown in. It was bound to explode.

Yellow Saunters Down The Aisle

Yellow's whispering grows louder approaching the stage. . . . Enron and WorldCom are simply larger manifestations of the sordid underside of the New Economy and of the business world I witnessed daily around me. One too many Concorde flights finally burst the bubble. Disillusionment and dissolution run rampant. A dot-com veteran— once the darling of the business community—becomes an overnight pariah. Friends

It was a toxic concoction: one part "change-the-world" and one part "fuck the establishment," with one part "yeah, a condo in Vail would be sweet" and a dash of hubris thrown in. It was bound to explode.

still, the CEO and the CFO pass on my offer of coming with me to see *Startup.com* at the Sundance Film Festival. It's not a matter of having time to sit through a movie now—it's far too close to home. The CEO, a relocated Los Angeleno, is certain our tale makes an intensely dramatic screenplay—but, being shell-shocked, he doesn't have the wherewithal to bother. I wonder whether the founder, a millionaire before plowing his money into company #2, regrets abandoning the playwriting he pushed aside.

For some the existential questions began when they were no longer catnapping in cots in the server room (OK, I slightly exaggerate) but were filing unemployment claims. For others, they arose when they cashed in their founders' stock in the nick of time and realized they now had the millions to do practically anything they wanted if they only knew what that was. It is impossible to find a knowledge worker or creative class member totally unaffected by the NASDAQ market crash and the tech economy downturn. But plenty of opportunities to pause and reconsider our lives were on their way—including September 11th and its aftermath.

I moved to Silicon Valley in 2002 when everyone else was in mass exodus (no, not that Exodus—its empty buildings still stand off Highway 101). It no longer reeked of the get-rich-quick air of 1999. A mature sobriety was the rule. The frontier spirit of Po Bronson's *Nudist on the Late Shift* is replaced with the reflective questing of his ensuing *What Should I Do With My Life?* Something was bound to come out of this change in mood. I yearned for the authentic energy of possibility and self-expression. But Silicon Valley, an Indian entrepreneur reminded me, is one of those rare places where people can understand why you would choose to forgo a paycheck in one of the priciest places on earth in order to pursue a dream.

Enter Yellow Front And Center, Climbing Onstage

While scattered individuals have exhibited a decidedly yellow perspective for decades, Slashdot, Linux, and the new online media and collaborative workspaces—blogs and wikis—signal hints of yellow "by design" processes and media. (A yellow system does not mean that only yellow mind-sets congregate; yellow prefers to absorb ideas and concepts from any source in the palette.) And new media usher in new thinking—the act of using them breaks old neurological patterns and adds new ones.

In *Word of Mouse: The New Age of Networked Media*, Jim Banister points out that the Internet emerged as the first medium to emphasize feminine traits, or what Daniel Pink refers to as right-brain "R-directed thinking" skills. (Interestingly, research says men rank and women link. The blogosphere ranks and links.)

The blogosphere represents the first medium to integrate both the masculine and feminine: a truly androgynous mind-set. And integration isn't a combinatory function but a fusion. More akin to soup than salad.

Preceding blogs, the Linux operating system was an early hint of yellow-by-design processes. One could imagine a sort of free-for-all democratic process behind the success of Linux. If Torvalds had gone with that strategy, the end result might resemble that hideous painting Vitaly Komar and Alexander Melamid produced, inspired by a poll of 1,001 Americans' view of good art: a landscape featuring George Washington, a strolling family, deer, and a hippo thrown in for good measure. Left entirely to the whims of voting and consensus, works of art, software, and even brands lose their cohesion.

"How do you get customers fired up about a new product in a tired category? Simple. Turn your brand over to them," says a March 2005 *Fast Company* article on Jones Soda Co. Not so simple in actuality. In the same article we hear Chris King of Jones Soda Co. say: "The customer's not always right. F——- that. If you're always trying to cater to everyone, you have no soul."

So Linus Torvalds and a very closely held circle hold the reins of Linux's soul. Ultimately it's up to them to make the final call of what's in and what's out—and while each contribution may be considered, not everything is accepted. When Torvalds opened up Linux for collaboration he was already starting with a vision, the kernel of the operating system. Kernel: the seed he'd envisioned and planted. That's not exactly to say that Torvalds owns Linux, either. It's closer to a dialectic between what green might deride with a smirk as the "Linux elite" and its community.

Before Linux, software companies created their proprietary products behind closed doors and, in a similar vein, corporations told their story to mass markets via mass media. And it was their story.

Then customers (and a few fringe marketers) started countering: Hey, it's our story. You don't own the brand. Alex Wipperfurth defines brand hijack (a phrase he used as the title for his book) as a synonym for consumer takeover or "the consumer's act of commandeering a brand from the marketing professionals and driving its evolution."

Whether you are on the I or you side of the "who owns the brand" debate, both are about wresting control: a battle of who's right—orange or green? What if one got above the turf wars and could survey the battleground from a higher vantage point? And what if it wasn't even a battle? (If you do one thing as a result of reading my words, read Chapter 12, "Telling the WE Story" in *The Art of Possibility* by Rosamund Stone Zander and Benjamin Zander.)

Now What?

I wondered about the inner workings of open source software projects such as the Linux operating system for a long time. You couldn't get me to code for free, I said. Why would anyone? I realized we obviously had different motivations, yes. Yet I couldn't quite put myself into their shoes. I kept exploring and questioning, and years later I finally understood the open source worldview because I embraced it, shared it, encompassed it: I was blogging for free.

The research literature would lead you to believe you simply cannot comprehend another viewpoint, period, if you've not encompassed it yourself. Starting in infancy, people go through the whole Graves palette beginning at survival beige and moving on to more complex shades. Most of us tend to stabilize at the value-meme currently in vogue in our environment—influenced by our parents, our locality, our culture. That is, unless the constellation of beliefs that make up the value-meme isn't operating well in our lives and we seek alternative answers.

Unfortunately, although we aren't conscious of it, we're all a bit like autistic children. That is, we suffer from varying degrees of mindblindness: inability to relate to others from their perspectives.

Here's an example of mindblindness in action: In one experiment, autistic children are shown a familiar candy box and asked, "What do you think is in here?" They say, "Candy!" But the box turns out to contain pencils. When asked what a new child who comes into the room will think is inside the box, they reply, "Pencils." And they're also certain that they always thought the box held pencils. Unlike normal children, they can't seem to conceive that beliefs can be false and that two people can hold two different and potentially diametrically opposed beliefs.

Along with the advent of new media and new thinking, the opening of worldwide markets ushers in fragmented, oft-conflicting worldviews. The business stage is crowded with players of all persuasions—each heeding separate and distinct director's instructions. The research conclusion: If you can't encompass my perspective, you can't understand my perspective, and thus you can't ever understand me.

Although the literature frames the model as a map of the evolution of human consciousness, what it really gives us is a map of the evolution of human concepts. But, ultimately, we are not the current constellation of sense-making concepts. We are not the beliefs we've inherited from our tradition, our culture, our society, our parents, or our religion. We're not even the beliefs and stories we make up about ourselves. The woman I know who over time has shifted from atheist to evangelical Christian is exactly the same person. She didn't dissolve, but her beliefs did.

That's the good news. The bad news: Adults assume. I assume you are like me, or like something I know. You assume the same of me. We may know that others are potentially coming from very different worldviews, but we're mentally geared to trust our assumptions because they've worked just fine, mostly. Maybe. Until now.

More bad news. According to the literature (and my empirical observations), although we've each lived in many different parts of the palette, we diss the neighborhoods we've come from. Say maybe I once resided in blue before I moved to orange, and now I'm swimming happily in green. I understand blue. Hey, I've been there. But it's stifling in the blue. And it's way nasty and lonely in orange. We tend to devalue perspectives we don't hold any longer. We get carried away at times and view people as their worldviews. Thus, they feel judged. Sadly, we can never truly communicate with those we judge.

Once we get to yellow and beyond, things brighten up again. Yellow marks a transition into value-memes that can relate to those nested below. And what is most important, it respects and values their contributions with far less judgment.

Honing the skills of empathy and empathic communication is the solution to this quandary. In a 2004 webinar with Daniel Pink, management guru Tom Peters cited empathy as the most crucial of the six skills that Pink, a *Wired* contributing editor, outlined in *A Whole New Mind* as essential in the future global talent markets. Empathetic communication is the fifth habit listed in Steven Covey's classic, *The 7 Habits of Highly Effective People*.

However, what we're all most adept at is conceptual empathy, that is, scanning for a frame of reference we can personally identify with. But what if there just ain't any such animal? Conceptual empathy isn't sufficient when the concepts are out of your league. What you need is a higher, more general view. Nobody looks down from an airplane and points out the window exclaiming, "Oh, look, there!! See the dotted line separating India and Pakistan?" You simply don't perceive borders from that vantage point.

When water joins with water, it is not a meeting but a unification.

—Swami Prajnanpad

Blasting Assumptions

A new reader stumbled across my blog and later in his own blog described me as a "New Age Californian."

I wonder what conclusion he'd have reached if he knew that the day before, between meetings in San Francisco, I'd ducked into a bookstore to read *Forbes* magazine's annual billionaires issue. Or what he would make of the fact that I'd lived in the election-map "red states" of Utah and Florida for twenty-eight of the last thirty years? Or that I'd moved to Silicon Valley two years earlier to work on business plan due diligence with some colleagues who broker deals between venture capitalists and early start-ups. Ah, then would I be a bourgeois capitalist?

He was scanning his repertoire of worldviews and frames of references to quickly assess: was I green or orange? This or that?

We all do this all the time—and rather insidiously. One of the functions of the brain is to filter and pattern match. This thing is a table—it doesn't present new information. No need to process its texture, the craftsmanship, the grain of its wood, or to touch this particular one. Table, check, done. Anthony de Mello, a Jesuit priest and author, tells us that our ideas can become a perceptive barrier to reality. We cease to see a table and rely on our ready-made concept of tableness.

Marketers are simply notorious for this: we segment and slice and dice the population and make broad-ranging assumptions. On the furthest extreme beyond quick categorization, people believe that marketers literally lump customers into one category, as this statement attests:

In this age of test-marketing and spin, here is a business that does not treat the customer as a credulous cash dispenser.

—*Inc.*, speaking of craigslist

You can study value-memes until you are blue in the face. You can read up on and focus group Latinas, women, Baby Boomers, Gen Y, Harley-Davidson devotees, *Star Trek* fans, or any other imaginable demographic and psychographic under the moon. Ultimately these methods yield zilch in terms of real comprehension. I've been in those focus groups—and rarely do I come away feeling understood. I'd settle for being heard.

We make up stories about groups of customers to simplify our lives. Unfortunately, these simplified stories are based on our own autobiographies and what we're familiar with. We don't know what we don't know.

One of the most challenging skills in the world has got to be seeing things from another perspective—the customer, the employee, the partner, the supplier, the person sitting on the other side of the table—because we are constantly filtering everything through our own perspective and making unconscious leaps about others based on our perspectives, our decision-making framework, our autobiographies, our experiences with others beforehand, and our frame of reference.

And so when a new customer comes in the door, or sends e-mail, or sits down for the one-on-one interview, are you interacting with your mental story or are you listening and directly experiencing that person? How much of the time have you plucked up an idea from the trusty story grid in your head and scarcely needed an interview for validation?

With a personal story idea firmly in hand, the mind is off and racing again: Now, what's a great story to tell to a New Age Californian? Sustainably grown crystals and sage? Bonk! Try again. You don't know me well enough if you think a New Age story works on me.

Before concocting stories—and many marketers are fairly proficient at creating, telling, and spreading stories—it's useful to take a refresher course in observation.

That's observing versus thinking—what Buddhists call bare attention. You note, register, and observe what's arising moment by moment. You're not thinking "about," not needing to do something "with," and—most important—not comparing or putting things in relation to anything else. This skill, which psychiatrist Arthur Diekman calls deautomatization, is the goal of all contemplative traditions.

Observation is especially key at the fuzzy front end of marketing—at the innovation stage. Even more cost draining and time consuming than the wrong sales pitch is an entire product built on the wrong premise.

The Human Frame Of Reference

It's hard to believe, but you can go to the hinterlands of Papua New Guinea, and tribesmen there would correctly recognize the emotions captured in face shots of Italians, Americans, and Iranians. In other words, they instinctively know the basic emotions of anger, sadness, fear, surprise, disgust, contempt, and happiness. The August 5, 2003, issue of the *New York Times* describes how researcher and psychology professor Paul Ekman did just that, to prove we hadn't culturally adopted a set of expressions by watching Charlie Chaplin and John Wayne. Ekman says, "[The tribespeople] not only judged the expressions in the same way, but their posed expressions, which I recorded with a movie camera, were readily understandable to people in the West." (See the story headed "The 43 Facial Muscles That Reveal.")

Being a lifelong photographer, Ekman naturally chose visuals as his tool, but he emphasizes that "voice is absolutely just as revealing." Once we come across a person, a story, a way to make sense of the world, or a marketing campaign that is beyond any shared frame of reference we've encompassed, the thing to do isn't to give up or to judge but rather to drop into the human frame of reference—a common ground that runs under the radar of the conceptual.

Almost intuitively, great brands have hit upon themes that resonate universally and connect to this common ground. Starbucks offers a classic study of recognizing the human frame of reference—the pull of a social "third place," a home away from home. And Red Bull is another such brand, defying heftier rivals PepsiCo and Anheuser-Busch as Alex Wipperfurth points out in *Brand Hijack:*

> The company has been incredibly successful, both over time and across geographies, in standing for something broader and more flexible: energy and stimulation. The result is that Red Bull can mean different things to different people. . . . From truck drivers to clubbers to extreme sports enthusiasts, Red Bull weaves itself into the lives of very different groups of people without ostracizing any of them. It effortlessly crosses socioeconomic boundaries.

Kevin Roberts, CEO of Saatchi & Saatchi, tells the story of a highly successful television advertising campaign for Telecom New Zealand featuring scenes portraying the bond between fathers and sons. He's shown the TV spot in hundreds of presentations and makes the following observation in his book *Lovemarks:*

> In Dubai, Denmark, Los Angeles, London, New York, Sao Paulo, Barcelona, and Sydney, the response never varies. People feel this spot is talking to them personally. The story makes a deep emotional connection.

In *Wild Mind: Living the Writer's Life,* Natalie Goldberg shares a story one of her friends wrote about someone dying of AIDS. It ends by saying, "Jeff was a doctor. The nurses stood crying at the nurses' station because they believed a thirty-three-year-old doctor should not die." Thinking of the piece, she notes:

> There is a quiet place in us below our hip personality that is connected to our breath, our words, and our death. . . .

> I could take Miriam's . . . piece to Asia, to a small village there, maybe a place that knew nothing of AIDS, and they would understand her writing, because it came from the place where we are not American, not gay, not a New Yorker.

But if we wipe out country, sex, religion—the things that form us—where does writing style come in? Style is all these things fully digested into our humanness, so the fact that Miriam was brought up in New York doesn't overrun the basic emotion of sorrow.

Once we come across a person, a story, a way to make sense of the world, or a marketing campaign that is beyond any shared frame of reference we've encompassed, the thing to do isn't to give up or to judge but rather to drop into the human frame of reference—a common ground that runs under the radar of the conceptual.

At the human frame of reference, we share a common motivation. The Dalai Lama says, "I believe that every human being has an innate desire for happiness and does not want to suffer. . . . Though some of us have larger noses and the color of our skin may differ slightly, physically we are basically the same. The differences are minor. Our mental and emotional similarity is what is important."

The basic desire for happiness and to love and to be loved can be viewed as the mountain peak motivator. How we choose to we get to that peak is where our beliefs and worldviews differ; each has its own path to the peak. Evidenced by footsteps on the path, people all sincerely believe that theirs is a viable and good route to the peak.

While one person sees a Lear jet parked in a private hangar as the path to freedom and happiness, another might chose sculpting clay figures each morning outside the door of a roving RV. Our worldviews have much more to do with the how (to get there) than the what. Happiness is the root motivator that binds all the worldviews.

The Conversations We Are Not Having

Among [Darwin magazine author Graeme] Thickin's reasons [for disregarding blogs]. . . . Business doesn't do passion; business doesn't like gossip; business doesn't like doing public experiments; business doesn't bare its soul; business writing style and blogger style don't even come close.

Each of these arguments falls at the first word; the fanciful notion of a single, monolithic thing called "business." Well, this imaginary creature may not like passion, or gossip, or public experiments . . . but people do, and that's probably why the numbers of bloggers keep growing.

—Johnnie Moore

Nike, P&G, Intel, Saatchi & Saatchi and countless other firms embed themselves within their customers' environments much as anthropologists study a foreign tribe or culture. Hitting the mark on both the product front and the brand (symbol) front requires a firm foundation in actually knowing your customers' stories. And that starts with a bit of "deep hanging out"—and perhaps a conversation or two that doesn't skirt around the customers' burning issues.

Companies scramble to find out what matters to their customers and what makes them tick—all the better to sell to them. But business folks are typically left out of all these vital conversations. And why is that? It's impossible to hear your customers' burning issues and their stories if they sense taboos—conversations where they'd be judged for even considering the topic much less expressing their authentic feelings and viewpoints.

If "markets are conversations" as *The Cluetrain Manifesto* asserts, an awful lot of intensely important conversations aren't even being whispered about in the presence of business.

I'm not speaking of the internal and unsaid "let's tiptoe around the elephant in the room" conversations that plague all companies. More precisely, I'm talking about the conversations that get to the heart of the matter for your customers. Even if those conversations seem completely (debatable, but I'll humor you . . .) irrelevant to the tangible product at hand—they are where emotional resonance, universals, and the brand reside. At the end of the day, no matter what industry you are in or what you are selling, the bottom line is your customer is ultimately . . . a person.

We are embarrassed by sex. We'd rather not think about death. And if we bring up God (or god or gods), noses will get out of joint. Yet sex, death, and God are the most profound considerations of mankind. How can companies hope to remain relevant if they won't discuss them?

—*Harvard Business Review*, February 2005

Sex, death, God—the stuff of human conversations.

Astonishingly, nearly every one of my friends is an engineer or scientist by training. Unbeknownst to me at the initial meeting—at a ski shop or a running club, no matter—they'll later announce themselves to be, surprise, nerds too. The most rational, analytical people in your workplace—yes, even the guy with a couple of patents in digital encryption or the one who runs the strict quality assurance for the lab or the physicist in the high-energy accelerator—yes, even they think and talk about these very human subjects. A lot.

These are the deepest aspirations of human beings, aspirations for immortality—that is, for an experience beyond time and space, for we are the only beings that are aware that we shall die. Even if we are good scientists, we know we are going to die. The diversions we create for ourselves cannot prevent us from thinking of the fact that sooner or later we shall die. No diversion can prevent us from that truth.

—Seyyed Hossein Nasr

Your blog is the "deepest" one I read, two different readers recently told me. At a lunch meeting the aforementioned QA manager (entirely unprompted) differed, saying, "You haven't written anything profound in a while." Months before, he'd said that if he had his own business he didn't see much need for consultants, nor executive coaches—ah, but a spiritual adviser, that'd be different. He compared our face-to-face conversations with what I'm writing for public consumption, and I had to admit I hold back.

The truth is we are all holding back more than we can bear. The dam is bursting at the seams—people are yearning to talk about what deeply matters to them. And there's hardly anyone around willing to listen. The conversations we most want to have are hushed behind closed doors—or they're not happening at all. War, says a Croatian woman I met in Italy, has made Croatians more openly conversant about life matters. Yet she is convinced that the United States is the hotbed of spiritual discussions because so many New Age and spiritual bestsellers spring from American authors.

"What about the best-selling *Celestine Prophecy*?" I tell her I have no idea where those purportedly millions of readers were—perhaps they're all closet readers. We don't discuss these matters in polite company. Or, that is to say, in business.

After a one-day writers workshop I went out to dinner with a few of the attendees—all complete strangers, as they say. We delved with intensity into the amazingly intricately interwoven topics of sex, death, and God. What started out as a breezy comic discussion on writing erotica quickly went to the bone. Two sisters shared their father's last words ("I'm ready to come to you") and how they've grappled with death and God since. Another woman's voice quivers as she shares the ups and downs of taking one day at a time while she and the husband she clearly loves very much cope with his Parkinson's disease. Yet another reveals how her own buried grief rose up when a best friend lost his wife.

I don't bring up death now from a sense of overriding grief or morbidity. But death has a particular way of bringing a stark focus to the fragility of life. And what's important in life. (In other words, what's important to customers.) A friend recently shared that her marriage separation took shape after her sister's unexpected death at the age of thirty-eight. "I looked at my life pretty closely after that."

That's the appeal of mega-bestsellers such as *Tuesdays with Morrie* and *The Purpose-Driven Life*.

These conversations may all seem anomalous. But I can assure you they are not. They are simply human conversations. I'm surrounded by these kinds of conversations all the time. And I'm just a marketer—not a clergy member, not a nurse or a doctor, not a counselor, not a therapist, not a masseuse, not a psychiatrist, not a social worker, not a coach. Simply another human being willing to listen without judgment, with compassion—and that's enough.

Tuning Forks

Our limbic system, the emotional brain we share with all mammals, is a powerful antenna, attuned to each other's wavelengths. When we say, "My heart went out to him," we're saying we can't help but resonate, even when we try not to notice.

—Marc Ian Barasch

Beyond the conceptual empathy we're most familiar with, there's resonant empathy. Often it's in the pauses within a conversation that true communication occurs. UCLA research cites that words themselves (or concepts) influence listener impressions the least. Facial expressions, body language, and the quality, tone, pitch, variation, and volume of the speaker's voice accounted for 93 percent of the impact of the message.

Lorne Ladner relays a tale his wife, Terry, tells of working at an upscale department store's cosmetics and skin counter in his book *The Lost Art of Compassion*. An irate older woman stormed in one Valentine's Day to return a container of eye cream she had purchased, screaming at the young, attractive employees that the stuff plainly doesn't work—"Look at my eyes!" Terry explained that it was no problem to return the eye cream, and the woman huffily threw the receipt at her. In a split instant, Terry noticed something beyond the stated words and surface emotions.

> "Your eyes are very puffy today. Is everything all right?"
>
> The woman retorted, "No." There was a long pause during which neither of them moved. . . . Somehow, as they looked at each other, they experienced a moment of genuine connection there in the midst of a mall. The woman softened. Though she certainly hadn't known it when she came in, this was exactly what she was looking for—a connection.
>
> She said, "Really, I've been crying. Every night, I've been crying. You girls don't know what it's like to be getting old, to be alone. It's just terrible." Her eyes welled up with tears. Empathy had uncovered the loneliness beneath the anger, allowing for a deepened sense of intimacy.

In this exchange, Terry wisely used resonant empathy to surmise that more was percolating under the surface. Whether we are trying to understand individuals or markets, we can easily brush past carefully buried issues and deep-seated motivations.

I had an enlightening encounter recently. A woman railed about being discounted as a woman. She was tired of the corruption she'd witnessed firsthand in her workplace to the extent she no longer trusted anyone in business or government, but particularly those of a male persuasion. She was so vehemently bitter and angry with the oppressors crushing her she was shaking when she spoke.

Conceptual empathy allows us to take the statement and state of mind—"I'm angry at being taken advantage of and feeling like a pawn"—and relate it to our own similar experiences and states of mind. We don't have to necessarily fully agree with the cause-and-effect, we simply conceive of the state of mind. This approach is the most commonly used tool in empathic communication, but it has its drawbacks. In this case, as with the irate cosmetics customer, there was much more to the story.

Resonant empathy works when we're clearly responding to something going on in the other person that's vibrating within ourselves. Terry at the cosmetics counter noted how, immediately following the tense energy of anger, the next emotion that arose within herself was sorrow. This led her to ask, "Is everything all right?" In my own encounter, I was experiencing the resonating fear of being vulnerable although many others in the same group only perceived the obvious tough stance and rage. Once I recognized this, I felt an instant flush of compassion and recognition, and the entire conversation shifted 180 degrees.

PRACTICES

Over the last few years, I've gone from being self-conscious and uncomfortable with people to being equally at ease with Nicholas, the homeless Vietnam vet who frequents the parking lot of the neighborhood coffee shop, and with Thomas, the savvy biotech executive seated next to me on the direct business-class flight to Paris. When I look back, I'm startled to realize that I've honed only two practices in the process of this transformation. They have made all the difference in both my personal and professional life. Neither is particularly difficult; neither is particularly simple.

Some say that empathy cannot be taught, but it can be learned.

Dismantling Walls

Marketing people talk about emotion. They present charts and diagrams, even raise their voices and wave their arms, but fundamentally they treat emotion as . . . out-there, felt by someone else and able to be manipulated. Analyzing other people's emotions and refusing to acknowledge our own dumps us in the same old rut. What a waste.

—Kevin Roberts

PHUKET, THAILAND, 27 December 2004: I lay weeping into my pillow at 4 A.M., curled on a green vinyl-covered twin bed in the fully lit hospital rehab room. The nurses attempted to muffle their chattering and the tsunami news streaming from the TV around the corner was turned down low. Were they OK? And what of the gypsy families on Koh Jum we saw near the boat bar weaving their nets and fashioning bamboo squid and shrimp traps days before? What of the Danish family in the bungalow closest to the sea? What of every single person that donned one of the Santa hats that Phen, the bungalow operator, passed out at the Christmas Eve party? I shook the thought. Yes, yes, they must be fine.

The unparalleled depths of sorrow, grief, anguish, and despair that rose like an angry sea dragon in the hours, days, and weeks that followed threatened to consume me even as the tangible tsunami did not.

At times like this we are tempted to draw up the bridge and fortify the walls, where in fact the thing to do is seize opportunity—while the heart's soft spot is palpable—to further crack open the fortress walls that keep us distant from others. This was the first time in my life that the temptation to run from intense emotions didn't win out. I didn't "let go" of feelings—rather the pithy advice was "let be." I simply rode the waves out. I sat with whatever came up without resistance and surprisingly I learned that the way out was through. Buddhists concertedly cultivate their capacity for empathy via openheartedness, or *bodhichitta.*

Fortunately for us, the soft spot—our innate ability to love and to care about things—is like a crack in these walls we erect. It's a natural opening in the barriers we create when

The unparalleled depths of sorrow, grief, anguish, and despair that rose like an angry sea dragon in the hours, days, and weeks that followed threatened to consume me even as the tangible tsunami did not.

we're afraid. With practice we can learn to find this opening. We can learn to seize that vulnerable moment—love, gratitude, loneliness, embarrassment, inadequacy—to awaken bodhichitta.

—Pema Chodron

Strangely enough, I've found that my ability to remain present to pain, grief, and sorrow has made me less hooked by these emotions; I'm able to withstand others' dramatic outbursts and intense expressions of suffering without triggering unresolved emotions within myself. Meeting our own intense emotions without resistance allows us to skillfully and gently handle others' emotions without our own getting in the way.

Recently I witnessed a woman standing at a church service topple right over. She was having a seizure. While a doctor ran over and paramedics were called, I found that my presence of mind was uncharacteristically unwavering in its calmness and loving healing thoughts extended outward without thinking. Normally, I'd be more panicked and worried. As spiritual teacher Sakyong Mipham Rinpoche noted after the tsunami tragedy, "We want the suffering to go away because it scares *us* or it causes *us* personal pain" (italics mine). Our own anxieties and fears, along with ignored and frozen emotions, come back to the foreground of our memory. Thawing out can be painful, but I wouldn't choose to go back to the tundra of numbness.

Empathy can become second nature. The facial photographer and researcher introduced earlier, Dr. Paul Ekman, developed another test measuring how well someone can read people's emotions from watching a videotape of rapid-fire, fleeting changes in expressions and attempting to correctly identify the emotion. This test's results are known to correlate with empathy. Most people do very poorly, but two Buddhist meditators in the study received nearly perfect scores.

One of the two monks, Matthieu Ricard, was shown a film clip used in psychology tests to trigger and elicit disgust. The clip was of severe burn victims having dead skin carefully, painfully stripped from their bodies. When one has cultivated openheartedness in repeated practice as Ricard has, it's not surprising that rather than the self-referential anxious and reactionary response of disgust, he felt "caring and concern, mixed with a not unpleasant strong, poignant sadness." Ricard insists he is not an extraordinarily gifted monk—in fact, compassion and empathy are the entire point of practice. The Dalai Lama has said he does not practice a religion so much as he practices loving-kindness.

Chances are, you will not be in a tsunami. But any day you're facing a separation can open your heart up to others located anywhere in the globe who are facing similar relationship endings and feel lonely, scorned, confused, or any other emotions that you are feeling. The day you go to the ATM machine and discover you're down to your last ten bucks, you may suddenly feel your heart lurch out to those millions that contend with poverty on a daily basis. Whether you are in a minor car accident, lose a pet, go through a layoff, struggle with your teenager's drug problem, file bankruptcy, lose a best friend to cancer, or any number of tragedies large and small, it's an opportunity to connect with the soft spot within and wedge into the hairline crack to further dismantle the wall that separates you from others. You may only have a few opportunities—use them wisely.

As our technology becomes more sophisticated we perhaps think that our emotional responses need to be more sophisticated as well. But what seems best is simple, direct feeling that is not padded with logic or twisted concepts, such as, "Maybe they deserved it," or, "I'm glad it's not me," or, "They should have known better," or even, "That's their karma." These contorted responses reflect poorly on our own state of mind. If compassion feels unnatural, it's probably because we're still thinking of ourselves.

–Sakyong Mipham Rinpoche

Besides riding out the waves of emotion, I've been practicing metta—the meditation for cultivating loving-kindness and compassion that monk Ricard uses. It begins with extending loving-kindness toward ourselves, then moves out in a circle to mentors and those who've supported us, then further on to loved ones, then strangers, and then even those we dislike (advanced practice!) until the loving thoughts extend to every sentient being in the universe. "It's compassion with no agenda, that excludes no one," says Ricard an interview with Marc Ian Barasch in *Field Notes on the Compassionate Life*. "You generate this quality of loving and let it soak the mind."

I can envision a cloud of loving-kindness starting at beige seeping out to the next encircling purple Russian doll, then to the red, to blue, to orange, to green, to yellow, to turquoise, to coral, and infinitely spreading out to encompass the whole range of worldviews until they collapse into white.

Polishing Walls

They went to their room
and began cleaning and polishing the walls.
All day every day they made those walls as pure and clear
as an open sky.

There is a way that leads from all-colors
to colorlessness.

—Mevlana Jelaluddin Rumi

The first practice of dismantling the walls through cultivating opportunities to open the heart is an advanced practice. We're lucky to peek through any of the tiny fissures. But while the walls are up, we can at least keep them shiny, clean, and polished.

I treasure the work of the thirteenth-century Afghan Sufi poet, Mevlana Jelaluddin Rumi. His *Chinese Art and Greek Art* is a favorite of mine. A king is settling a debate about who are the best artists with a contest. "The Chinese suggested then that they each be given a room to work on with their artistry, two rooms facing each other and divided by a curtain." The Chinese artists proceed to paint an elaborately intricate colorful mural with a hundred shades of dye on their wall. The Greeks never touched a single dye. As the snippet that opens this section states, the Greeks spent entire days polishing the wall. The detail and colors of the Chinese mural "astonished" the King. Then the Greeks pulled back the dividing curtain to reveal:

> The Chinese figures and images shimmeringly reflected
> on the clear Greek walls. They lived there,
> even more beautifully, and always
> changing in the light.

A good marketer allows the customer's reflections to shimmer purely without distortion. Our filters don't distort; our perceptions don't skew. We simply become like a mirror. No, you can't possibly juggle all the varied pigments of concepts. What you get when you overlay every single color isn't completeness—it's opaque darkness. Black. The absence of colored pigment is white. White Greek walls perfectly reflecting.

In *A Brand New World*, Scott Bedbury (who was director of corporate advertising for Nike) recounts how Nike had hit a growth plateau. The internal debate around extending the brand beyond the original die-hard athletes to the broader fitness category hit a stalemate.

Having been a committed marathoner, I know that there is a couch potato lurking in the most serious of athletes. It's a shadowy figure we keep at bay. We tend to have disdain for that which we loathe—even mildly dislike—within ourselves. I imagine it must have made a few folks in the original athletic core of Nike wince when weekend warriors, baby-pushing joggers, and mall walkers were now considered as potential prospects.

Finally one ad campaign spoke to both the founding core of Nike's employees and clientele and to the expanding fitness category. "Just Do It" was inclusionary—pro athletes, aging weekend warriors, and even a dog out for a walk—were featured in TV spots. "The deep secret to the longevity of "Just Do It" lay in the fact that its message possessed as much relevance for twenty-year-old triathletes as for fifty-year-old mall walkers," Bedbury continues. "'JDI' was not uniquely male or female, not just sports-or-fitness-oriented, neither purist nor recreational. It embraced all categories."

Psychologists use "the shadow" to describe the parts of ourselves that we've buried in our unconscious and neglected out of fear of disapproval. When we run across some-one or something that evokes any memory of this shadowy part within ourselves, we "project" the shadow outward onto them. We tend to exaggerate our perception of the trait within them—whether or not it's even present—just because they've triggered its remembrance.

Nike had to confront its wimp/loser shadow before it could expand into the fitness category. Paradoxically, "Just Do It" resonates with the indomitable hero tucked in all of us; this unifying message bridged the two groups while subtly acknowledging the shadow.

Shadows obscure large swaths of brilliant whitewashed walls. Usually shining a light evenly on the wall dissolves the illusory darkened splotches.

The fundamental skill of observation comes back into play. This is the single most indispensable practice: watching thoughts and feelings from a distance, much as a meteorologist watches the changing weather patterns go by—without judgment. That includes the particularly tricky practice of observing your judgment—both your self-judgment and your judgment of others—again, without judgment. Simply notice. (We can never practice enough radical self-acceptance.) It's because we "project" precisely those unloved, unwanted, self-judged, and self-loathed aspects onto others that self-acceptance is crucial. And that's why metta begins with extending acceptance and loving-kindness to your own self first. The unaccepted are merciless. We believe that the darkened hues in the shimmering images displayed on the walls of our perception are actually in the original rather than our own shadow obstructing the reflection. Both conceptual and resonant empathy are unreliable when your projections obscure your perception of the world.

In addition, simply note how other people push your buttons and particularly your strong likes (guru- and goddess-worship, pedestal-plopping, admiration, adulation, awe) and dislikes (annoyance, contempt, disgust, dismissal). (The overtly positive traits are typically disowned as well.) Notice judgmental comparisons you make between yourself and others. Every person I encounter becomes a chance to show me my own blind spots (the shadow lurking below).

As you can learn to recognize and then recall your own projections on the wall, you will no longer need to make forced attempts toward compassion and empathy. You will see the other person's reflection as clearly as your own. Eons before the wall is spotless, you will experience rich connections with others. Willingness, not mastery, is enough for dramatic results.

CONCLUSION: MY MARKETING PHILOSOPHY IN A WORD

I suspect these practices may at first glance sound like horrendous drill exercises. "Be curious" has been my motto ("Ah, that's an interesting reaction . . ."). Curiosity transforms the onerous into the intriguing and illuminating. As conceptual empathy fails us with alarming frequency in the future, we'll more naturally be inclined to be more curious.

Ironically, these touchy-feely practices do alter neural pathways. Over the long haul they lead to the cognitive abilities that Clare Graves noted in the subjects most able to enlarge their "perspective intelligences," including agile decision making and an ability to engage and tackle systemic problems freshly.

And the outcomes go far beyond the cognitive. Matthieu Ricard "soaked his mind" in the unconditional compassionate glow of metta meditation while ensconced in an fMRI machine measuring his real-time brain processes. The experiment, by neuroscientist Richard Davidson, showed Ricard's brain had intense activity in regions associated with joy and enthusiasm. In fact, the scan of his brain state was entirely off the bell curve dotted with 149 other participants' results—pegged furthest, by far, on the happiness meter.

The benefits accrue to your customers and prospects too. "There is no method, no program, and no technology that can make up for a lack of love for unbelievers," says Rick Warren, author and pastor of the largest church in the United States (acknowledged by *Forbes* magazine as a business in its own right). Warren states that it is this all-encompassing love (plus, naturally for a church, the love of God) that motivates and ensures his Saddleback Community Church's astonishing growth.

I typically don't state my personal marketing philosophy so bluntly as I have here. Ultimately, it is simply this: Love attracts. The word love gets twisted around quite a lot. Loving-kindness more aptly conveys the infusion of a gentle kindness with no agenda, no strings attached, that excludes no one and resonates at a fundamental human frequency.

Oh, and one more thing. You could drop the extraneous and simply say it as a verb: Love.

FROM THE EDITOR

Evelyn. . . . I am not quite sure where to start. When I was formulating *More Space*, she was the first person I asked to join our merry group. I felt the project needed her take on the world. If you read her blog, you'll find it hard to classify. I think the best things in life are those that are hard to categorize. If you are looking for Evelyn, you'd find her in the proximity of Apple Computer's corporate headquarters (in California).

In Her Own Words . . .

What is it about your essay topic that made you want to write this chapter in *More Space?*

"Ultimately, I think Peter Drucker's statement frames my essay:

> Society needs a return to spiritual values–not to offset the material but to make it fully productive. . . Mankind needs to return to spiritual values, for it needs compassion. It needs the deep experience tat the Thou and the I are one, which all higher religions share.

Empathy and the capacity to transcend the "us" versus "them" barrier isn't a pithy blog post topic. Even 10,000 words merely scratches the surface."

Evelyn's blog:

evelynrodriguez.typepad.com

Evelyn's favorite blogs:

www.gapingvoid.com

www.jorydesjardins.com

www.johnniemoore.com/blog

Recommended reading:

No Boundary
by Ken Wilber

The Art of Possibility
by Rosamund Stone Zander
and Benjamin Zander

A Brand New World
by Scott Bedbury

Passion And Entrepreneurship

----

by Curt Rosengren

When I think of successful entrepreneurship, the notion of passion inevitably comes to mind. The word immediately brings to mind people so over-the-moon on fire about what they're doing that they can't sit still.

In my work—helping people identify their passions and create careers that ignite them—I've seen again and again the incredible difference tapping into passion can make. For this essay, I wanted to take a look at how that same passion plays into entrepreneurship, so I started contacting successful entrepreneurs and posing the obvious question: "How important is passion to entrepreneurial success?"

I might as well have asked them, "How important is breathing to success in staying alive?" The unanimous answer was, "I don't see how success is possible without passion."

Passion is the essence of the entrepreneurial spirit. It is an entrepreneur's fuel, providing the drive and inspiration to create something out of nothing while enduring all the risks, uncertainty, and bumps in the road that that entails.

Entrepreneurs' lives consist of a nonstop mission to communicate their vision and inspire others to support their efforts. As evangelists, salespeople, fundraisers, and cheerleaders they need to breathe life into their vision while enlisting others in their dream. From creating a vision for the future to selling the idea to investors, from attracting high quality employees to inspiring them to do what nobody thought possible, that passion is a key ingredient.

Passion also plays a key role in their belief that they can achieve the so-called impossible, bouncing back from failure and ignoring the chorus of No that is inevitably part of the entrepreneurial experience.

Robin Wolaner, founder of *Parenting* magazine and author of *Naked In The Boardroom: A Ceo Bares Her Secrets So You Can Transform Your Career,* put it succinctly when she said, "To succeed in starting a business you have to suspend disbelief, because the odds *are* against you. Logic is going to stop you." Passion, on the other hand, will help you fly.

WHAT IS PASSION?

Before I go any further, I want to clarify what I'm talking about when I say passion.

Because it's not something that is easy to put a finger on, passion often gets cast in a mysterious light. In reality, it's a very simple concept:

Passion is the energy that comes from bringing more of YOU into what you do.

Simply put, it's being who you are. It's taking off the mask and doing what comes naturally. It's following the flow of what you're drawn to, what energizes you, and what makes you come alive.

Think of your work as water moving from one place to another. The difference that passion brings to the picture is like the difference between trying to get water up and over a mountain and allowing that water to flow along its natural path in a riverbed.

Can you get the water up and over the mountain? You bet. You can design the pipeline, build the pipeline, and put constant energy into powering the pump that will push the water up and over the mountain. That takes a lot of effort, and when you run out of energy to power the pump, the water stops.

Contrast that with allowing the water to run its natural course. Rather than requiring outside energy for its movement, the water actually gets energy *from* the fact that it is following that course.

It's the same thing with passion. By tapping into what comes naturally, what lights you up at a core level, you are tapping into an abundant, renewable source of energy that you can aim at creating success. On top of that, you aren't wasting energy by focusing on things that drain you.

HARNESSING THE POWER OF PASSION

Strangely, in spite of its clear importance, very few entrepreneurs consciously incorporate passion into their decisions, ultimately leaving one of their most valuable assets on their path to success largely to chance. Why don't more people consciously tap into its power and potential? Partly because there is no clear, commonly defined way to do so.

The approach outlined in this essay has its roots in the nature of each entrepreneur as a unique individual. Few people would argue with the idea that entrepreneurship and passion go hand in hand, but where does it come from? What does it look like? The stereotypical view of what entrepreneurial passion looks like has a lot of basis in reality—the juice that comes from seeing something take shape out of nothing, for example. And yet for each entrepreneur there is room for an individual twist.

Each individual entrepreneur also derives that feeling of passion from different things, and has the potential both to sculpt what the business looks like and to shape a personal role in building and running that business so as to mirror the things that provide energy and excitement. No single job description covers the title of *entrepreneur*. That's the great thing about running the show—you get to decide what it looks like. That doesn't mean that an entrepreneur doesn't need to do what it takes just to get the job done. It means that all entrepreneurs are presented with scores of choices over the course of developing their businesses, and with an awareness of what lights them up, they can make some of those choices based on what will move them in the direction of passion.

The key question for any entrepreneur shouldn't be just "Do I have passion?"—it should be "How can I develop my passion even further?"

TOPICAL PASSION AND ELEMENTAL PASSION

When most people think of passion, they think in terms of what I call *topical passion*— being passionate about a specific subject like technology, empowering children, or baseball. For entrepreneurs, it might also be vision behind the company they are building, whether that's the problem they are solving or the revolution they want to start.

Is building a business based on a topic you feel passionate about a good source of passion? You bet! If you're on fire about the basic focus of what you are trying to achieve, it can't help but create positive energy. But it's not the whole answer. If you are working with subject matter you're passionate about, but the day-to-day routine consists of activity you loathe, it's going to lose its luster.

Topical passion can come into play when deciding what kind of company to found, but once that is set in motion it becomes a static piece of the landscape. The real opportunity to tap into your own unique and individual passion on an ongoing basis comes from another source: what I call *elemental passion*.

Elemental passion comes when the fundamental elements of what lights you up at a core level are present in the work you do. To consciously incorporate elemental passion into your work, all you need to do is dig in to the things you love (work *or* play!) and ask yourself why you love them.

Passion And The Bottom Line

It's worth noting that passion doesn't just have benefits for the individual entrepreneur, it can help the whole business thrive. Studies clearly show that fostering passion and engagement in employees has a significant impact on the corporate bottom line.

Gallup has been on the forefront of measuring the impact of what it calls employee engagement. Engaged employees are those who are performing at the top of their abilities and happy about it. According to statistics that Gallup has drawn from 300,000 companies in its database, 75–80 percent of employees are either "disengaged" or "actively disengaged."

That's an enormous waste of potential. Consider Gallup's estimation of the impact if 100 percent of your employees were fully engaged:

- Your customers would be 70 percent more loyal.
- Your turnover would drop by 70 percent.
- Your profits would jump by 40 percent.

Job satisfaction studies in the United States routinely show job satisfaction ratings of 50–60 percent. But one recent study by Harris Interactive of nearly eight thousand American workers went a step further. What did the researchers find?

- Only 20 percent feel very passionate about their jobs.
- Less than 15 percent agree that they feel strongly energized by their work.
- Only 31 percent (strongly or moderately) believe that their employer inspires the best in them.

Consciously creating an environment where passion is both encouraged and actively developed can yield an enormous competitive advantage. That environment starts at the top.

The Personal Impact Of Passion

Being an entrepreneur is inherently about taking the road less traveled and venturing into the unknown. The biggest sales job in any entrepreneur's path isn't selling to customers or investors; it's internal. Entrepreneurs have to believe in what they are doing—and in their ability to make it happen.

Richard Tait, one of the most passionate people I have ever met, is a great example of the power of that belief. When Richard founded the Seattle-based game company Cranium with Whit Alexander, conventional wisdom would have told them not to do it.

Looking at his decision to defy that conventional wisdom, Richard points to passion as a driving force. "This sense of passion has led me to have the confidence that you just don't have to take no for an answer. I constantly change the rules. I love to tackle big problems and figure out how to solve them. The game industry is dominated by two massive companies. If you go down the checklist of businesses that a pioneer should try to go into, games—especially my kinds of games—is not one that you would say,

'Yeah, that's a great idea. Put everything at risk to go and do that.' And it takes a lot of confidence and conviction to say, 'OK, yeah, I'm going to do that.' Passion gives me the confidence to be a pioneer."

Richard notes that it wasn't as easy as it might sound. "When we started the company," he remembers, "no one but our wives gave us the support to follow our dreams. It was the darkest and bleakest moment of my life in terms of emotional support, just needing someone to give us a thumbs-up and say go for it. Everyone, including the guys from Pictionary, told us we would be crazy to get into this business. But somehow we took the leap, we trusted every bone in our body, and clung on tight. To this day I still look at Whit and know that we took the equivalent of a business free fall and jumped off when everyone told us it could not be done. Passion was our parachute."

Since Cranium was founded in 1998, the company has met with consistent large-scale success, making history by winning the Toy Industry Association's Game of the Year award three years running.

There's something to be said for flying in the face of conventional wisdom.

Overcoming Fear, Uncertainty, And Doubt

When we see people who have accomplished great things, it's easy to put them on a pedestal and imagine they must have gotten there on a magic carpet ride, with no fears or doubts along the way. The reality is that I've never met anyone who did anything great without encountering fear. Erik Weihenmayer, the blind climber who reached the summit of Mount Everest in 2001, puts it this way, "If you think you're going to do something big and exciting without fear and doubt, and without worrying that you're making the wrong decision about a hundred times a day, you're being unrealistic."

When you're truly on fire about what you are doing, it overpowers the voices of doubt, both the ones inside your head and the ones belonging to others. Your passion drowns all the voices out so they don't distract you.

Gary Erickson is the poster child for how passion can trump fear and doubt. In 2000, Erickson was set to become rich with his half of a $120 million sale of the company he founded and co-owned, Clif Bar, (maker of one of the most successful energy bar brands on the market). There was just one problem—he couldn't do it. It didn't feel right. He had too much passion for the company, the people, and the product. In a last minute decision Gary walked away from the sale. Not only that, he financed an additional $80 million (including interest) to buy his partner out.

Industry experts predicted failure. Clif Bar's competitors had been bought by deep-pocketed mega-corporations. Few people thought the company had a chance standing on its own.

Looking back, Gary compares the fear he felt in the months that followed to climbing experiences he's had that scare him more now in retrospect than when he was climbing. "When I was on that rock, I was so in love with the moment and the passion of being in the mountains. And the passion of that moment outweighed the risk and the fear." His love for what he was doing at Clif Bar had the same effect. Five years after the almost sale, Clif Bar has grown from a $40 million company to $110 million today.

With passion as your driving force, you find a motivation and drive that helps you make your way over or around fear and doubt. The energy that comes just from doing the work propels you past obstacles, and fears often dwindle in the light of passion.

Tolerating Risk

Risk averse? Forget being an entrepreneur. Risk is an inherent part of the game. The ability to accept it is a key ingredient. Luckily, feeling on fire about what you're doing makes the risk involved in any new venture easier to tolerate.

Risk is a vital piece of the entrepreneurial equation, not just because of the risk-reward factor but because risk (and failure) brings with it a greater potential for learning. Tahl Raz has a bird's-eye view of the entrepreneur's world as a writer for such publications as *Fortune, Small Business,* and *Inc.* magazine. He suggests that the knowledge needed for success has less to do with learning a specific set of instructions (the well-documented mechanics of operating a business) and more to do with the subtle insights one gains through experience. Tahl calls this knowledge gained by experience *tacit knowledge.*

"Tacit knowledge, as opposed to the formal knowledge obtained from books, is the un-articulated rules and information of how to get things done that can only come from doing," Tahl notes. "And because entrepreneurs don't work within any preordained systems—they are creating and manifesting an idea within their own heads—that's precisely the knowledge that proves most important. And the most profound lessons in tacit knowledge, says Tahl, are learned through failures, big and small.

"Entrepreneurs have to have a good relationship with risk, and be willing to engage it." With risk inevitably comes some failure, and with it learning. "But all that newfound knowledge means little if it is not utilized, which is where passion comes in. It allows entrepreneurs to recover from failure."

Interestingly, a recent study by Wharton doctoral student Brian Wu asserts that entre-preneurs aren't actually more tolerant of risk than the rest of the population—they sim-ply have an inflated belief in themselves. They believe that they have a greater chance than most of succeeding. Thinking back to the discussion about the impact of passion on confidence, that makes a lot of sense. Of course, that also means entrepreneurs face a danger of deluding themselves and taking foolish risks, so passion must be balanced with logic and good judgment.

Persistence And Perseverance

The road to success in the business world is littered with the wreckage of failures whose sponsors simply gave up too soon. An entrepreneur's path is almost guaranteed to be bumpy—even hair-raising at times. It's easy to get disheartened when things get chal-lenging. It's easy to give up when things don't unfold as planned or grow as quickly as anticipated.

Passion can bring a relentless stubbornness to the picture that won't let you quit. It can be the driving force of dogged determination, encouraging you to grab hold and not let go until you've succeeded.

It is a source of motivation for the long term, a vital element in persistence. Passion generates an intrinsic motivation that can't be duplicated by external rewards alone. As Gary Erickson puts it, "If all we were trying to do was make a buck here, I wouldn't be very passionate about that. And I don't think our people would. That story gets old really fast. In every company I've seen that's chasing the dollar, at some point people just lose their passion for it. Life is more than just money. We all have to have money to live. We all need to pay our bills and eat. But at some point the excessive drive for more and more becomes a dead end, and people lose passion if that's all they're chas-ing."

SELLING THE DREAM

Entrepreneurs may be at the helm, but they don't travel alone. Their fire for what

Interestingly, a recent study by Wharton doctoral student Brian Wu asserts that entrepreneurs aren't actually more tolerant of risk than the rest of the popula-tion—they simply have an inflated belief in themselves.

they are setting out to do is vital for enlisting others in supporting the dream. As Alex Knight, a management consultant who spent many years as a venture capitalist, puts it, "Passion's important—particularly the ability to infect others with the entrepreneur's passion. Building something new and great is a difficult, irrational task. Passion is what gets people over the irrationality of what they're trying to do."

Entrepreneurs need to communicate an intangible energy as much as the actual substance of what they have to say. Their words can be eloquent, polished, and refined, but without energy your impact is lost.

For all the care we put into choosing just the right words to convince others, in reality they are only part of the package. Both body language and how we say those words play a large role in how they will be received. With passion as the driving force, your message naturally shines through in a much bigger way.

Passion And Investors

Passion is a must when pitching to investors. Yes, you need a great idea with a substantial upside and great people to make it happen, but it's passion that sucks them into the excitement of what you're doing.

Janis Machala, a management consultant who focuses on early stage ventures, has seen dozens of companies go through both successful and unsuccessful fundraising efforts. In her view, passion plays an enormous role, especially in the early stages of a company's life. "Investors are sharing in a dream," says Janis. "They have to believe the money will be well used against insurmountable odds—and there are always insurmountable odds. In the early stage it really is the dream you're selling."

She has seen an entrepreneur's passion (or lack of it) be the key to getting funding or not. "I've seen so many companies with a great story struggle to get funding because their founder doesn't communicate that willingness to walk over hot coals to make the dream happen."

Janis points out that emotions play a role in investment decisions, particularly with angel investors. "Especially if they have been entrepreneurs," she says, "they get caught up in the emotional component. They want to be part of that dream."

She also highlights how passion indirectly paves the way for funding success. "Passion can attract others to the dream. Advisers, board members, co-founders. People you look at and say, 'How did they get *that person* involved with them?!' Part of an investor's decision is based on who else is involved."

Mike O'Donnell, president of StartUPbiz and founder of several start up companies that were successfully grown and sold, relates his own experience with looking for funding. "I've raised a lot of money, both for my own ventures and other people's," says Mike, "and I can tell you, passion is the single most crucial attribute the entrepreneur can have. In every instance, the investor said, 'I was moved by your enthusiasm. I was moved by your conviction. You made a believer out of me.' And that's what gets them to want to be involved in the deal. It's not necessarily the plan, or the size of the opportunity. They all justify it based on those other factors, but the thing that hooks them is the entrepreneur's passion, or conviction, or enthusiasm. That's what moves people. Money does not move people. It just doesn't."

Mike stresses that passion can't be manufactured, it has to be authentic. "It can't be hyped," he says. "People spot hype like crazy. They can spot false passion. They know when it's B.S., and they know when it's real." But if it's real, he says, "it moves through the room. It's contagious. It's exciting to see."

Potential Partners

As an entrepreneur, your odds of having ready access to everything you need to make it happen are next to nil. Partnerships with larger, established companies can be a great way to get access to what you need to make the dream a reality. Whether it is for access to a distribution network, expertise, manufacturing abilities, marketing clout, or even simple credibility, smart partnering can help take the dream to the next level.

For the little guy just starting out, getting the attention of established companies and finding a reason for them to partner with you can seem like an insurmountable obstacle. One of the factors that can work in the upstart's favor is passion.

When Kevin Salwen and Anita Sharpe, both *Wall Street Journal* veterans, started the new magazine *Worthwhile*, they knew that distribution was going to be a vital part of making it fly. "If you don't have good distribution," says Kevin, "you're not going to get the circulation you need." They also knew what the Big Four newsstand distributors were likely to tell them: "We don't do launches." Still, they were determined to try.

They went to each of the Big Four, fully expecting that none of them would say yes, and made impassioned pitches. Three of them did say no, telling them to come back when they were bigger, but one, Warner Publishing, said yes. Kevin recalls, "They said, 'The concept is good, and the passion is great. We're going to take a risk with you.'" That risk started to pay off right from the beginning. The first issue of *Worthwhile* had a higher national sell-through than the average of the top twenty-five magazines.

Rajesh Jain founded India's first Internet portal, IndiaWorld, and sold it for US$115 million. On his blog, he looks back at the early days and reminisces, "As I went and met various content providers, it was this passion which helped me make them see the future of the Internet and see me as someone who was just the perfect partner. For those brief moments size mattered little. It was one person to another person. It was one entrepreneur to another entrepreneur. Making people feel that they can make a bet on the person across the table, however audacious the idea, is what passion can do."

Passion alone won't do the trick, of course. But it will definitely work in the entrepreneur's favor.

Employees

Most entrepreneurs don't start with a bankroll to dangle in front of prospective employees, but that electric vibe—what people feel when they see entrepreneurs on fire about an idea and what they're doing to make that idea a reality—inspires a strong desire to be part of that dream.

Gary Erickson looks back at the early days of Clif Bar and shakes his head in wonder that great people were drawn to work there. Thinking of one of the earliest employees, he reminisces:

> Our desks were in a cold warehouse where, when it rained in the winter, the water would flood in and we would have to move things around. We had these little heaters that you'd plug in that you'd electrocute yourself if you weren't careful. Thinking back, why would he want to work for us? What was it? I think there was this grassroots connection with what we were doing. He got it. He saw something. He saw that it was different. That we were scrappy. That there was some energy going on in that warehouse, that little 1500-foot-square warehouse, that was electric.

It wasn't the reality that engaged people, it was the energy and the possibility that people saw.

There was definitely a passionate draw toward the company, and when they walked into the little office, they were like, "Whoa, this is happening! This is going somewhere!" It's like a van of hippies coming by, and going, "I don't know where you're going, but I want to get in there." That's what it felt like in the early days.

Not only does passion draw employees in, it also has the potential to inspire them to go above and beyond. That intense belief coming from the leadership is contagious; it can ignite a similar belief and commitment in employees working toward that vision.

Gary Erickson's experience at Clif Bar is a great example. In 2000, when Gary pulled out of selling the company and took the helm of the demoralized, faltering company, industry experts were skeptical about the company's chances for success. And, at first, so were Clif Bar's employees. Gary describes the scenario:

> I walk in and I'm on fire, and these guys are in a lifeboat trying to paddle to shore. And the thing that saved us was passion. It wasn't, "Here, I'm going to give you a list of how we're going to make it. If we do this and this . . . " Because they didn't believe it. They didn't think we could make it without either selling to a company or getting some capital. Now I'm telling them not only are we going to make it, we have this big debt to pay off too, and I'm not taking any investors to pay off the debt. We're going to make the money to pay this debt off.

> I think people saw it in my eyes. I said, "If you want to be on this ship, let's go. If you don't, get off. I'll find people that want to give this a shot." And everybody stayed.

> Five years later, we grew from $40 million to $110 million now. We're more than halfway to paying off the debt. People were telling me in the days and weeks after I took the company off the market that they didn't know if they could rally again. And I was incredibly passionate about this company. I was putting it all on the line, and they knew it. I find it amazing how much that emotion, and that drive, and that passion turned people around, and we rocked!

Remember the statistics I talked about under "Passion and the Bottom Line"? It's all about creating a culture where passion can take root and grow, and any company's culture starts at the top.

The Balancing Act

Don't get me wrong. Passion isn't an entrepreneurial panacea. Not only does passion need to be coupled with a good idea, it also needs to be coupled with business acumen and the ability to implement. Without that, passion is like a fire hose with nobody holding on to direct the flow—blasting water in all directions with lots of energy but no real results.

At the end of the day, either the people with fire and vision need to possess that business orientation, or they need to bring others in who do—and then be willing to share the power and control.

Ideally, the keepers of the passion and the keepers of the logic have a symbiotic relationship that allows a company to thrive. As Lee Travis points out, "It's good to have a balance. You get too many entrepreneurs together and you'll probably save the world in twenty minutes. And then you need a bunch of logic-minded people to tell you how it can't be done. Somewhere in the middle lies the truth."

Not only does passion need to be coupled with a good idea, it also needs to be coupled with business acumen and the ability to implement. Without that, passion is like a fire hose with nobody holding on to direct the flow—blasting water in all directions with lots of energy but no real results.

One way to make sure those blue-sky tendencies don't get out of control is to make a conscious habit of doing a reality check with the people around you. Mike Apgar, founder and CEO of the broadband Internet company Speakeasy, describes his approach. "I have a lot of ideas. And they're not always good," he says with a chuckle. "There are people I use as a litmus test. Because of who they are and how they look at the world, I might trust their reaction to a given perspective of my idea, not necessarily the whole idea. Sometimes it's a room of eight people and I've got my full crew there vetting an idea. I'll look at each one for a response. I don't need everybody to agree, I just need certain individuals to give me a positive response on the aspect I trust them to understand and judge."

Mike also turns to the light of reality that numbers can give. "I tend to be an idea person. I like creative thinking. But then my very next thing I do is to apply a rigorous process to run those ideas through business modeling. And the most effective tool for me is to put the numbers into an Excel spreadsheet and be extremely conservative."

Finally, you need an ability to focus on the right things. Looking back on her entrepreneurial experience, Robin Wolaner of *Parenting* magazine talks about the endless possibilities an entrepreneur encounters. "Focus is absolutely important. I don't think you get it done without it. There's never enough time to focus on everything in a start up, so you need a way to focus on what's really important and not get distracted by the stuff that isn't."

IDENTIFY YOUR PASSION CORE

Earlier in this essay, I defined passion as *the energy that comes from bringing more of YOU into what you do*. So what exactly does that mean? How do you bring "more of you" into what you do? This is where the idea of elemental passion comes into play.

By distilling your passion into basic elements, you can consciously and systematically make choices which will bring that feeling of passion into what you do and keep it there. The concept is simple; if the elements you have identified are present in the work you do, you will likely feel on fire. If they're not, you will likely feel disconnected and unmotivated.

In my work of helping people identify and create careers that light them up, I have developed a model I call the *Occupational Adventure Guide* to help simplify the process. The model is based on the paradigm that your career is a journey. At the heart of that model is the passion core, the internal compass that points the way toward a passion rich career path.

Because our culture focuses so heavily on action and results, most people don't have a very well developed internal compass. They don't know what lights them up at a core level, what feels truly meaningful and gives them energy. So they turn to an externally generated compass to tell them what direction to go. Unfortunately, that external compass often has nothing to do with what makes them feel energized and engaged.

Elemental passion is the passion that comes from doing something that is rich in the elements that form your unique passion core.

Identifying your passion core gives you a way to consciously bring elemental passion into the picture. It takes a distinctly heart-focused concept—passion—and puts it into a format the brain can wrap itself around and understand.

Again, the idea is simple. It's about going beyond an awareness of the things you love doing and identifying the underlying characteristics of why you love doing them. You and I can both say, "I love [something]"—I love travel, for example—and odds are good we're speaking two completely different languages. You might love travel because of X, Y, and Z, while I might love it because of A, B, and C.

Make a list of things you love doing. When you've made the list, pick one and start asking, "Why?" Why do I enjoy this so much? Why is it so much fun, so meaningful and so fulfilling? Typically you will come up with a handful of reasons. For each of those reasons, ask why again. Think of it as a reverse engineering process, peeling back the layers and identifying underlying characteristics. Inevitably, as you continue doing that for multiple things from your list, similar characteristics keep bubbling to the surface.

For example, I love travel photography. Why? Well, part of it is because it's about seeing new things. Why is that so appealing? Because there's an element of exploration and discovery to it. And why is that so much fun? Because something new is always just around the corner. And why is that important? It's the stimulation of the new. Truth be told, I have the attention span of a gnat, and the things that keep me interested and engaged tend to have frequent little discoveries along the way. When I look back on what I have really loved doing over the course of my life, work or play, 95 percent of it has had a strong element of exploration and discovery to it.

One word of caution, it's easy to stop too soon and miss out on many of the insights you could get if you kept digging. Challenge yourself to go down four or five layers of asking, "Why?"

Remember that the items on the list of things you love don't need to be work related, just things that light you up. The very first time I did this exercise with a client, the first thing he wanted to explore was the Skip Barber Racing School, which is one of those programs where you spend a weekend learning how to drive really fast around a track. My immediate reaction was, "Oh no! Shot down in flames right out of the gate! What are we possibly going to get that's relevant to his career out of looking at a racing school?" We ended up digging into that for a good hour, and there was an incredible amount of information there that applied to what lit him up in his professional career.

Putting It To Use

No single definition covers what it means to be an entrepreneur, and no single path presents itself for an entrepreneur to take. When you understand your passion core—those characteristics that are the underlying pieces of the things that light you up—you have a tool you can use to make decisions that consciously bring passion into the picture. If you haven't yet started a business, you can use it to help you identify both the business that's right for you and the way you want to approach it. You can tailor your approach to the company and your role in it.

Decide What Kind Of Entrepreneur You Are

When you have a better understanding of what lights you up at a core level, you can better evaluate what kind of entrepreneurship is right for you. Entrepreneurship can take a variety of shapes and forms, but to make it easy, I'll break it into two main categories, *high growth* and *lifestyle*.

We live in a culture where the focus is on *betterbiggerfaster*. As a result, we tend to think of an entrepreneurial venture in terms of creating a company that will grow and keep on growing. Scalable is the buzzword those in the know like to use. From the slick pages of business magazines to the costly seats in business school classrooms, high growth entrepreneurship is what we are taught to pursue if we want to be entrepreneurs.

But is that for you? Maybe, maybe not. Do you get a charge out of building something out of nothing? Tackling the impossible? Watching something grow (and grow, and grow)? Maybe the high growth version is for you.

On the other hand, if your interest lies purely in creating a business to suit yourself, you could be lifestyle entrepreneur material. This kind of entrepreneurship is focused less on maximizing revenue and more on creating the life the entrepreneur wants to live. Such entrepreneurs generally have few employees—and no designs on building an empire (I fall into this category). They can certainly be financially successful, but they typically aren't in it for the money.

Open just about any business magazine, and you will find plenty of examples of the up-and-coming high growth entrepreneur. The concept needs no further elaboration. Lifestyle entrepreneurship, on the other hand, has until recently gotten little attention. I'd like to point to a great example of a lifestyle entrepreneur, and how she used her awareness of what lights her up at a core level to envision and create her business.

Suzie Goldsher found herself feeling burned-out and depleted after leaving a successful marketing career with a regional grocery store chain. In the process of trying to regain her energy and figure out where to go next, Suzie hired a personal coach and worked with a variety of alternative healers. The change that the healing work has brought to her life is having a profound impact. "For the first time in my life, I feel like I'm thriving," she says. "There's a sense of joy, comfort, and peace." She looked around and, realizing that the people who had helped her so much were in dire need of marketing help—which just happened to be her area of expertise—she began to see a glimmer of opportunity.

At the same time, her work with a coach gave her focus on what she really wanted. "It was absolutely critical because of the clarity it gave me. Once I had that clarity, I carefully sculpted a business that would express my values and be a place where I could work with like-minded people." She saw the opportunity to blend her marketing knowledge, a lifelong gift for building community, and her desire to support the growth of alternative healers. The result is her company, Best Life Services.

Focus On What Brings You Passion

Everyone I talked to as I researched this essay agreed on the importance of focusing on what lights you up. Some gravitated to it intuitively; others learned it the hard way.

Over the course of his career, Dave Herbig, CEO of the Seattle-based start-up Badge Magic, has taken on a variety of entrepreneurial ventures. After a stint as the COO of a company that he helped go public, Dave left to look for new opportunities. He started looking at entrepreneurial possibilities, but somehow the fire had dwindled.

As he tried to figure out where the fire had gone, Dave looked back at how things had unfolded in the past and realized that he had taken too much responsibility for everything. He began exploring where his elemental passion came from and, as he did, saw how activities that he disliked and that drained his energy had taken up far too much of his time.

At the same time as he was taking steps to identify the parts of being an entrepreneur that really lit him up, Dave identified an opportunity and launched his new company. Badge Magic offers a product for easily fastening cloth badges to clothing. The company started with the Boy Scouts and has been expanding steadily ever since.

Dave was able to put his finger on the things that energized him and those that sucked him dry. Then he started building his business while maximizing the activities that energized him and minimizing those that left him feeling fustrated and drained. In this way, he has been able to focus on what comes most naturally to him.

"If you're doing what you love, you're you, and that's where flow happens," says Dave. "I think about that all the time. There's a constant awareness of where the fuel comes from. I focus on the parts that I do best, and look for ways to get rid of the things that get in the way. I've been able to tailor my entrepreneurial experience to how I function best." The result is more productive, high-energy time spent on building the business.

Mike O'Donnell of StartUPbiz regrets not having made his decisions from the core earlier. He ultimately realized that "the title on my business card was wrong," an affliction he sees affecting many young entrepreneurs.

> Early on, I misread myself and my motivation because I was buying into the popular culture about what an entrepreneur is and what an entrepreneur does. And I find this in a lot of young entrepreneurs—"I'm starting this thing. I've got to be CEO." As I matured and really thought about what energizes me, I realized I hate being CEO.
>
> If you just check your ego, about this title and what society puts on it, if you take that out of the equation, you can get to the essence of where you live. Where your center is. And my center is not in being CEO. I thought it was, because that's what I was taught it was. But my center is really in being the Chief Evangelist, and pulling all the pieces together and lighting everybody else up. I'm really good at raising the money, firing up the investors. I'm really good at bringing in the people who are going to build certain pieces and maintain them. I'm really good at turning on the first customers because I'm passionate about it, but I'm not really good about being the guy who's having to manage everybody and write the checks every month.

Had he known what he knows now, Mike would have done things differently. "I probably would have tried to identify the maintainer," he says. "The Harvard MBA guy or woman who is really good and gets off on that part of the business. But at the time my ego wouldn't let me be called anything except for CEO."

His advice to other entrepreneurs? "Stick to what you're good at and what you love, even though society and ego and expectations and investors and all those other things revolving around are telling you you've got to do these other things as well, you don't necessarily have to buy into that."

Sculpt Your Existing Entrepreneurial Role

You can use your understanding of your passion core to bring more passion into the picture to ensure that you stay energized and engaged for the long term. Nothing is static. Things always have room to shift and change. Once you can put your finger on the source of your elemental passion, you can consciously begin to make decisions that will lead you in that direction.

Take a look at each of the passion elements you have identified in creating your passion core. Where does it match up with what you are doing in your day-to-day role with the company? What can you do to bring more of that into what you do? Where is your day-to-day activity out of alignment? What can you do to change that?

AVOID BURNOUT

No doubt about it, being an entrepreneur is hard work. It takes time and commitment to achieve success. The last thing you want is a feeling of burnout getting in your way.

Passion is a kind of renewable resource. Doing the work gives you passion, which in turn gives you more energy to do the work. It creates a positive cycle. By consciously integrating passion into your approach to entrepreneurship—and your life in gen-

You can use your understanding of your passion core to bring more passion into the picture to ensure that you stay energized and engaged for the long term.

eral—you can tap into a renewable resource that keeps you energized and engaged.

That idea is as applicable to your life outside work as it is at the office. The decisions you make about how you spend your time outside the office can either energize or drain you as well.

Dave Herbig came up with a great approach to make sure he was getting energy from all corners of his life. At one point, he realized that he had been so focused on his entrepreneurial efforts that he had stopped doing things in his outside life that energized him. He was no longer doing anything that made him feel "juiced." To counter that, and be sure that he was building the energy of passion into his life as much as possible, Dave created what he calls a "juice menu." He made a list of activities that he really loves doing and made a commitment to pick one thing from the juice menu each day and do it.

Make A Habit Of Listening To Yourself

If there is one thing you can do to tap into the full potential of passion, it's making a habit of actively listening to yourself and acting on what you hear. You are the single best expert in what energizes you and leaves you feeling engaged. The minute you start making decisions based on anything other than what lights you up at a core level, you risk veering off the path.

In this culture, we're not conditioned to listen to our gut, our intuition, but time and again I've seen people hurl themselves headlong down the wrong path by basing their decisions on external considerations rather than on what was right for them at the heart of the matter.

Robin Wolaner found that out the hard way. The founder of *Parenting* magazine says that the worst decision in her career came when she let ego rule her decision to accept an opportunity as CEO of *Sunset* magazine after Time Inc. bought *Parenting*. She grappled with the decision and ultimately took the job. Looking back now, she realizes that if she had made a list of pros and cons when considering the choice, even the items in the positive column would all have been externally based and ego driven (things like higher visibility, bigger company to run), having nothing to do with what really made her happy. She ended up being miserable in the job. Had she consciously asked herself, "Will this make me happy, or am I making this decision based on external factors," she would have avoided that.

Find a way to listen to yourself. Journal. Find someone who will really listen and not just spout their own vision of what you "should" do. Meditate. Hire a coach. The more you can slow down and listen to yourself, the better your decisions are going to be.

Reality Check

In an ideal world, the work we do would be all passion, all the time. But the reality is that there will always be parts of our work that we don't enjoy. As Lee Travis says, "There's probably 20–30 percent of my time that gets dragged into stuff I don't like, and that's just part of being the CEO of the company. But the fact that I get 70 percent of my time doing the stuff I really like, that's what makes me get out of bed and run in here first thing and get crankin'."

The key is to consciously make decisions to maximize what lights you up and minimize what doesn't. Lee observes, "If you're an entrepreneur and you're a Type A control freak, then you have a tendency to micromanage and want to control the details yourself. But then you have an internal conflict going on between what you want to do and what you are doing. You want to do all these passionate things, but you keep doing all these things you don't like to do because you have to be the control freak. I hear a lot of entrepreneurs complain about the stuff they don't want to do, but then they won't let go of it. And so it creates an internal conflict."

Here's a simple idea that can pay off in spades. Take a look at your role as an entrepreneur and ask yourself two questions. "What do I love about what I do?" and, "What do I dislike?" Keep it somewhere that you will see it regularly. Make it a habit to look for ways you can do more of the former and less of the latter. Slowly, over time, the percentage of your day dedicated to what you love will increase, and the percentage spent on what you don't will be whittled away.

To both succeed as a business and keep that passion alive, you may need to give up some of the pie. Lee Travis looks at it this way. "A lot of entrepreneurs go out of business because they ignore the necessary but boring things, and that's where things like partnerships make sense, or key employees, or stocks. Because as an entrepreneur I would rather give up something, not have to do the part I don't want to do, and grow the company to be that much bigger. Meaning," he adds with a laugh, "I'd rather own a smaller piece of a bigger pie than 100 percent of the small pie and have to do accounting."

NEXT STEPS

Ultimately, passion comes from you, and no one else. At the end of the day, tapping into its potential is about answering the question, "What is going to make me feel energized, alive, and engaged?" By understanding that, and making your decisions and choosing your path accordingly, you can consciously tap into that energy to fuel your entrepreneurial success.

So what now? Here are some steps to get you going:

- Explore the source of your elemental passion by creating your passion core. Make a list of things you love doing (work or play) and ask yourself Why? Ask it over and over, until you get down to the basic truth.

- Take a look at your existing role. Where does it match your passion core? Where is it out of alignment?

- Make a list of ways you can bring more of what lights you up into your day-to-day activity.

- Begin making a list of ideas for ways to get rid of what is out of alignment. Implement one.

These are just a few of the next steps you should take. For a complete list visit www. astroprojects.com/morespace/curt.

FROM THE EDITOR

Curt's blog:
blog.occupationaladventure.com

I found Curt the same way I think many do. I was trying to figure out what to do next. His blog "Occupational Adventure" is a constant source of inspiration for those trying to find their path. Curt always talks about the importance of passion in your career. He calls it "the energy that comes from bringing more of YOU into what you do." Curt is living his life passionately near the Space Needle (in Seattle).

In His Own Words . . .

What is it about your essay topic that made you want to write this chapter in *More Space?*

"I saw that passion and entrepreneurship are inextricably linked, yet nobody has really taken a look at the effect passion actually has, and how it might be leveraged even further."

Curt's favorite blogs:

www.worthwhilemag.com

ming.tv/

www.worldchanging.com/

Recommended reading:

The Occupational Adventure Guide e-book: www.passioncatalyst. com/download/
by Curt Rosengren

Raising the Bar: Integrity and Passion in Life and Business: The Story of Clif Bar, Inc.
by Gary Erickson and Los Lorentzen

Naked in The Boardroom: A CEO Bares Her Secrets So You Can Transform Your Career
by Robin Wolaner

The Passion Plan at Work
by Richard Chang

Going Home

----

by Robert Paterson

Is this your life?

Imagine, you are lying on the floor in a corridor in your university. With so many students and so little space, this is what you do when you are tired. You have just left a class of two hundred other students. You have never met the professor. Your only contact with the teaching staff has been with a series of harassed TAs. You graduate soon and your nights of study are often punctuated with fears about what you are going to do. Your student loans are over $30,000. You will graduate this year with thousands of others who also have no job. Everyone told you that you had to go to a university to get a good job and to have a good life. What is wrong with that advice? You feel helpless. You feel betrayed.

Imagine, it is lunchtime on Friday. You are fifty-two years old and have just left the deputy's office. You joined the health and social services department all those decades ago because you wanted to make a difference. But for many years you have only been able to put the time in. You can barely remember when you did anything that really helped. Now all you can do is to try to keep the wheels on. You have just taken early retirement. You wonder what happened to kill your dream. You feel betrayed and you wonder if you also betrayed those you once sought to serve.

Imagine, it is three in the morning and the bar is empty except for you and the other members of the band. They are celebrating. You have been noticed. After years of grind in bars like this building a sound and a repertoire, you are on the verge of signing a deal. But as your friends celebrate, you are thinking about what the deal really means. You will become an indentured slave. All the power is with the company. Is this deal going to be worth it? After all your years of effort, the pay-off is to become a prisoner. You feel helpless. You feel betrayed.

Imagine, it is midnight and you have won your seat in Parliament. Everyone around you is jubilant—but you are depressed. You went into politics to make a difference. You thought that it would be all about the issues. But to win, you had to become a spin expert like all the others. Worse, you know now that you are good at it. The Prime Minister's Office has noticed you and is making warm noises about a cabinet appointment. You know that what they noticed was not your expertise or your passion for children and families but your big name as a sports legend. You feel helpless. You can't back out now and you will play the game. You feel that you have betrayed yourself. You wonder if you will now betray the country.

Imagine, you are in hospice in Charlottetown. You are scared. You look back at your life. You did all that was expected of you. You have been a pretty good husband and dad. You had the career that your father so wanted you to have. You did him proud, ending up a senior executive of a bank. But you are so sad. You are so sad. You always loved working with wood. After you retired, you discovered that you were a cabinetmaker. And what about Jean? She was your great love but you chose duty instead and backed away. Who have you betrayed most? You lived all those other people's plans for your life and you have missed your own.

Imagine the countless other stories: the bored schoolboy on Ritalin; the Pakistani doctor driving a taxi in Toronto; the laid off coal miner. Imagine the life of a teacher or a nurse today.

Imagine your own story.

We surely live in desperate times.

LIVING IN THE MATRIX

I think that we in the West have been asleep for a long time. An idea put us to sleep.

It was a hundred years ago that Henry Ford took the Newtonian idea of a machine-like construction of the universe and made it manifest on Earth.

Now we take it for granted that education is a linear process that leads to a credential. Now we expect that health care is an intervention by special people who deliver drugs and procedures. We take it for granted in business that we can have an economy or a healthy biosphere but not both. We take it for granted that work, family, and education are separate processes that compete for our time. We think that it is normal to have a job and a manager. We believe that having more things will make us happy. We accept that we have no real say in the governance of our workplace. Bombarded by millions of messages telling us what to buy, what to eat, what to wear and what to do, we have no confidence in our own innate judgment about what is good for us.

This mechanical model of separation has us gripped so totally that we don't even know that we live in a kind of Matrix—straight out of the movie. For most of the last century the success of the Ford model of mechanical relationships worked. The model delivered a massive increase in overall well-being in a material way. We no longer experience this model as anything other than normal.

But the price has been the loss of our humanity and a growing threat to the biosphere that supports all life. Now we are restless. The system does not deliver what we want anymore. It just consumes more of our energy. We don't know what is wrong but we know that something has been broken.

At this moment of despair, a new culture is awakening. This new culture is the child of Einstein and the revolution in physics of the early twentieth century.

I believe that "social software" is a vector for a return to an old culture.

When I say old culture, I mean the culture that fits the essential nature of humans and that fits nature itself. I imagine a return to the custom of being personally authentic, to a definition of work that serves the needs of community, and to a society where institutions serve to enhance all life.

This is surely good news, but I also fear that the road home will not be easy. Culture is tied into our identity. We do not give up our identity without a fight. A new culture is not then a new idea that can be sold by consultants. A new culture goes to war with the old in a fight to the death.

WHY HERB LAUGHS—CULTURE WARS

Why do Dell, Southwest, Starbucks, and Wal-Mart, who all share parts of the new culture, stand alone in their sectors? Why has there not been a rush to adopt their business model? Why are there not legions of consultants working with eager clients to jump on the bandwagon? It's not happening.

Dick Fosbury won an Olympic gold medal for the high jump by a foot. But you may be surprised to learn that other leading athletes did not rush to copy him, either. It took more than ten years for his technique—the "Flop"—to become standard. Why the delay when it was obvious to all that the Flop was decisively better than the old-style "Straddle"?

Imagine you have jumped using the Straddle for fifteen years. Your mind may want to use the Flop but your body will fail you as you approach the bar. It will try and Straddle as your mind tries to Flop. You will fail because your muscle memory is more powerful than your intellect. You cannot shake the habits of a lifetime. And it was not only the athletes who could not adjust. It was also the coaches. How can you coach using the Flop when your reputation has been built on the Straddle?

This is why Herb Kelleher laughs at his competition.

Herb laughs because you cannot buy your way into the new culture. You cannot will your way into the new culture. He is in a world that his competitors cannot reach. They are all trapped in the Straddle. Not only are his competitors trapped, so are most of those that advise them, such as the big consulting firms and the business schools.

You cannot argue your way into the new. People can see it or they cannot.

This is the struggle of perception that Howard Schultz (of Starbucks fame) had with his early owners. They saw the coffee business as being all about the transactional activity of selling beans. Howard saw it as being all about an emotional experience. They could not see what he saw. He had to leave to help them change their minds.

IBM sells its PC division. HP buys Compaq. Nobody copies Michael Dell's customer-driven process. Why? The idea of allowing the customer to drive the process is heresy for them. They would rather die than accept this idea. They will martyr themselves for their culture of control.

Think about Sears and Kmart. Sam Walton's huge idea was not about efficiency as an end in itself. He set out to listen to his customers and to give them what they wanted and not what he thought that they should have. So the polarity at Wal-Mart is from the stores to Bentonville, not the other way around. The guys at Kmart laughed. Who is laughing now?

I am not saying that all future success will be slavishly to copy Sam, Michael, Howard, and Herb. These are early days. The revolution has hardly begun.

So what side of the bifurcation are you on? Are you a Flopper or do you Straddle? One thing is for sure, I can never persuade you to change your belief by an argument. Like Galileo, I will do my best to show you instead.

BACK TO THE FUTURE

We are going back to the end of the Middle Ages.

Like now, this is a turbulent time. War has been constant. Plague has killed off a quarter of the population over the last century or so. A new world has just been discovered that is going to pump money into Europe and pull adventurers away. Islam has just been driven out of its last European holding. A tidal wave of social and religious unrest has been crushed utterly by an invincible combination of a universal church and a set of temporal rulers who are gaining in power.

More powerful than the sword of the king is the power of the media. The pulpit fills the role of today's mass media. It is the only source of information for the mass of people. Literacy is confined to the Church. Books are rare and very expensive. They are written in Latin or Greek. Knowledge is locked up. Not only does the Church control the processes of communication, it has a tight control on the message as well. Its two main messages are that salvation is only possible if you give the Church your total obedience and much of your worldly wealth—and that God himself has appointed the temporal rulers over you.

Then on 31 October 1517 Martin Luther nails his ninety-five theses to the door of a church in Wittenberg. At the heart of these theses was a big idea: people need no institution between them and God.

A hundred years later, in 1633, the Inquisition convicts Galileo of heresy. His crime was to use evidence to refute the dogma that the earth was the center of the universe.

These are powerful ideas. But when faced with all this power against them, they needed a viral vector to spread. With all this power lined up behind the establishment, open war would have been suicide. Only a virus could get through the immune system of the time.

The viral vector began humbly in 1455, at the Frankfurt Book Fair.

In that year, Johann Gutenberg sold the first copies of his mass-produced German language Bible. He sold them for three hundred florins each. This was the equivalent of approximately three years' wages for an average clerk. However, it was significantly cheaper than a handwritten Bible, which could take a single monk twenty years to transcribe. The viral vector was out and the ideas that it carried could not be stopped! The lock on communications was broken.

Who would have known then that a priest with a big idea, a man with a telescope, and a man with a new communication tool would come together to shake the world?

Can we see our own predicament in this light today? Is this not our pattern too?

Is not our great problem that the great institutions of our time—government, health care, education, arts and entertainment, even business—no longer serve us but only themselves?

Is this idea of going direct the same for us as Luther's big idea that man could talk directly to God? Is not the new doctrine for organizations based on the observable working laws and designs of nature the same as Galileo's observations?

Is not the enabling vector a new type of communication device that is so simple and so inexpensive that it will give voice and hence power back to individuals and to their communities? Are we not standing at the beginning of a new reformation? Has the wheel of history turned full circle?

Let's find out. Let's jump forward in time to the near future. Let's pick 2009 and drop in on how some of the pioneers in 2005 have done. Let's go to where I live, Prince Edward Island, my adopted home. Let's have a look at what might happen to many aspects of our society as the freedom of blogging works its way though our institutions and our current habits.

The Right Space

You are a leader in the Drupal Movement. You have just arrived in Charlottetown from Vancouver to visit your friends here. You have been developing the community education alternative to WebCT. Your toolset has become the new norm for an online university and, as Firefox broke though in the browser wars, so you too have broken through in education.

Will has picked you up at the airport and has delivered you to where you will stay, the Queen Street Commons.

You of course have your own version of the Commons, the Robson Commons, in Vancouver. In the last year The Commons Network (TCN) has erupted all over North America and in the United Kingdom. Like Visa International, the TCN is a nonprofit association that provides the connective tissue for thousands of local operations. With more than a million members and growing exponentially, TCN is now able to provide its members not only with a network of space but with the buying power to offer individuals the price of insurance and many other services that could never have been accessed by individuals. TCN is a vast network of free agents who now have the power of the network effect behind them.

Your Robson Vancouver membership has given you the right to stay at Queen Street Commons for $25 a night. It's like a home and not a hotel. It is clean and comfortable and, what is more important, it is full of your friends who spend a lot of their day working there. Your network is here. It is like going home but in another place.

The Queen Street Commons is a safe space that is designed to build trust and community. It is a physical eBay. It had some founders who set up the initial conditions but, as in eBay, the expanding community of members is taking it off into all sorts of directions that could never have been thought of when the doors opened in 2005. It is the very essence of the new worldview. It is a "generative space" that brings forth life from within and also replicates itself. It evolves into new forms as well that feed back on each other, changing all the time as new needs appear.

THE MEDIA REVOLUTION

The Commons has its own local radio station and TV, the PEI Broadcast Network. City Filter, the parent company of a large network of small town community newspapers, is also located at the Commons and is a partner of the PEI Broadcast Network.

This approach to local media is exploding around the world, and advertising revenues are shifting rapidly to the new medium as it gathers local support. This revenue shift started in classifieds but has now spread to the mainstream as context-sensitive advertising has replaced punting for consumers and as authentic word of mouth has replaced spin. The established global media system is in shock as it is eroded from the small local markets up into the national and global markets.

The most recent provincial election has just taken place and the PEI Blog/Media was central to the emergence of the PEI Party, which has nine seats.

What was different was the demise of the sound bite. With the new media, the issues were finally put on the table and candidates had to get engaged in a dialogue. Claiming that you were going to get more money for health care raised the question of "For what?" Then the answer of "To hire more nurses" raised the questions of "how and why?" Then the debate really started.

Voters and their MLAs were starting to debate why the schools were not working rather than all assuming that simply more money would be the answer. Now more people could see that the real energy issue was not the price of gas but of how best to become independent of the use of oil. Now many could see that more doctors and nurses on their own could not make us well. What many could see was that we all had to get re-engaged in our lives and in the lives of our communities.

Consequently, there has been an earthquake in political policy development. Education, health care, and energy policy are all on a self-help and community track now. There is a growing recognition that more of the same is not the answer. As new community projects come online and work, the remaining pool of doubters shrinks further.

The country watches. There is no going back to the sound bite and to being bribed with our own money.

THE NEW AGRICULTURAL AND ENERGY REVOLUTION

In 2005, the Prince Edward Island (PEI) Food Local Network was born. It had a simple idea. Like eBay, it would create a safe space where small local producers, using a distributed network, could offer their eggs, their hens, their pork, their grass-fed beef, and their organic veggies to their fellow citizens. Now if you wanted good food, buying it was easy.

The key was social software. Every farm has its own blog that is aggregated into the main site.

The prices were good for all as the middleman was cut out. It was convenient; the scale of the network assured that everything in season was available. Most important, it was trusted. When you bought a chicken, you knew that this bird had had a good life and was healthy. You knew who had raised it. You knew that in buying it, you kept the money in circulation on PEI.

A great initial stimulus for the new food system was the PEI school system. As part of the new health awareness, the Eastern School Board contracted the PEI Local Food network to supply breakfast and then lunch for the kids. Within two years the results in the schools and on the land were enormous. We had a breakthrough in obesity with the kids who also took their new diet back into their homes and we had enough of a market to drive the growth of the supply side too.

The new farm is once again the old farm. The ideal is to have forty acres of mixed crops. Farming is becoming a way of life again. Good food is becoming commonplace. Our rivers and our soil are showing signs of renewal.

Many of the larger industrial farmers have also found a new way. The survivors, led by a group in Kinkora, shifted their focus from growing commodity potatoes to growing energy. Now every community on PEI has a few turbines. It was a deal between the School Board and the local farmers that set this in motion. The School Board needed a hedge against $100/barrel oil. It had a two-pronged strategy. It created a market for biodiesel for its school buses and it created a local electricity customer for wind power. The communities built out from these centers. In less than six years PEI is well on its way to being independent of oil.

The supermarkets still do well but all can see that the new way will eventually, like Open Source in software, overwhelm them. With this powerful concentration of power being eroded, they are acting much more like Microsoft did as the advent of Firefox revealed its vulnerability.

The Health Revolution

The new health model is clear now. It started as an experiment for seniors on PEI. With help from the Federal government, a tiny project was launched in 2005 where a social networking tool was set up with a few seniors. The objective was to see what would happen if seniors were connected on the Web with each other.

Within two years, there were more than three thousand members and more than fifty groups on PEI alone, and the network is spreading all over North America.

Initially, the most popular groups were in health. The health groups grew up at first as support groups. The first was for people who had severe arthritis. Within months this group had become very expert. They were on top of the leading research and had lots of practical advice for each other. They provided not only moral support but also expert help. For a group for whom mobility was a challenge, the online aspect was a perfect fit. Many broke though their fears of the Web by taking lessons from other seniors in the Blogging 101 group.

Many who were disconnected from life now have a reason to get up in the morning again. The tracking research is showing us that the more connected the seniors were to each other and to the world, the better their overall health.

The University And Consulting Revolution

UPEI began an experiment in the summer of 2006. Come to PEI for the summer and meet the other students and then go on to take an online master's degree in the natural economy. The Master in the Natural Economy (MINE) is a master's degree course that engages the learner in as many of the ideas and practices of the new ways of organizing and acting as possible. It embodies the ideas of our new time. It draws on hundreds of gurus who live all over the world and bring their own stories and experiences to bear. Students, who nearly all are employed, develop their own path of study within the context of the course intention.

The school initially emerged out of one course, "Marketing as a Conversation," inspired by *The Cluetrain Manifesto* and by the ongoing thinking and blogging of people like Seth Godin, Hugh McLeod, Johnnie Moore, and Jennifer Rice. Their marketing revolution was the first breach of the old system that took hold.

Students can take any of a number of paths, but all the work is founded in the ideas of how real relationships and real networks work. Paul Hawken is dean emeritus, and the current dean of the school in natural economy is George Dafermos, whose early writing on the use of Open Source as an organizational model has been so influential. Robert Scoble is the Visiting Guru this year and will be on PEI this summer offering workshops in voice and culture. He replaces Dave Pollard, who will be sorely missed.

Students spend a month in the summer here on PEI, where their task is to get to know each other and to decide on their focus for study. They then return home and form groups that are facilitated by the gurus. The full master's degree costs only $7,000 and has no other costs. There are now seventeen thousand students in the system, which is four times the size of UPEI, a conventional undergraduate school.

MINE graduates are in extreme demand as organizations struggle to understand the shift that they have to undergo. The traditional business schools have had great difficulty in moving this fast because they have such an investment in the old. Similarly, the major consulting firms have all but collapsed, as they too could not reframe their costs and their competence.

In their place have emerged networks of gurus like Hugh McLeod's Hughtrain Alliance that is recognized as the key talent pool that shook the marketing world. These networks have a very unique model and become partners of the host organization. They are not report-writing organizations with expensive offices and extreme hierarchies but are much more like coaches of a team. Most MINE students use their studies to solve real issues at their full-time jobs.

In effect, consulting has become an extension of the education process.

The School Revolution

As with seniors, the revolution in PEI schools did not happen as a result of any deliberate transformation project. What is happening is that a series of projects designed to engage children have taken hold. This work did not even take place in the regular school day but in the afternoon.

The afternoon has become a place where children can do the one thing that they really love. The kids choose a favorite activity or subject area and then the community finds local experts to share their knowledge with the children.

This idea had its start in two areas, theater and sport. Theatre PEI began a community program in the afternoon to awaken kids to the thrill of theater. At the same time, Sports PEI began a similar program to offer the average kid more opportunities in sports. All this work was organized and expanded by the use of local blog sites that were designed to engage the local community. The resources came from adults who lived close by.

Now many other groups are filling the afternoon. The PEI Local Food Network has joined forces with 4-H to offer a successful program in growing and cooking food. Kids are learning the whole process from raising grass-fed cattle to slaughter and from butchering to cooking. It is now being seen as normal for people in the community to offer their help to kids at school. There is even a popular astronomy movement in the evening. We have all been surprised at the transformation of once bored children, who now are applying the kind of energy that used to be reserved for skateboarding to studying the night sky.

Overloaded teachers now have an army of allies and the schools have a new relevance as more and more is taught that makes sense to kids. The day curriculum, once so abstract, is rapidly moving to support the afternoon study. The astronomers drive a need for more complex math. The theater group drove a study of literature. Everyone has to be able to read. School is becoming fun.

GENERATIVE SPACE

I have only scratched the surface of what I can imagine. Can you see how each improvement in one place then acts to help another? In a network, every new node helps the whole. Imagine for yourself what can happen.

How different will be the experience of education, of government, of work, and of home lives?

So let's return to today. The two most important life-giving structures are in place: Google and the blog. These are both spaces in which life unfolds and then grows. They are interrelated and they support each other. They are both "generative spaces." It is their interaction that I believe will transform our world.

Let's start by looking at Google from this perspective of its being a generative space. What do I mean by this? How would you define Google? Does it act like a machine or does it act like an ecosystem?

How does Google make its choices about how to answer your search? It finds the answers ranked on authority. Google defines authority by a combination of page views and links. This is an evolutionary process where the world votes on value and the pages with the most votes rank first. This is how nature works.

Open Google News. You see a page full of news stories. There has been a choice as to what you see and this choice changes every minute of the day. What editor chose the stories displayed? There is no editor. The Google ecosystem selected the items.

Your Gmail from a friend mentions a vacation. On the right are a few ads for cottages. Unlike regular advertising, which comes at you for no reason other than your availability, these ads only show up when they are relevant. If you talk about food, food ads appear. If you talk about cars, car ads appear. Who selected these ads? The Google ecosystem allowed them to find you.

You are fed up with most ads anyway. Who would trust them? What you trust is the word of mouth of your peers.

Think of the billions spent on marketing today. In 2003 the U.S. carmakers spent $15 billion on conventional marketing. Only 15 percent of buyers made their choice because of this investment. More than 70 percent relied on word of mouth. Google will disrupt spin and place more value on word of mouth and on conversation.

Context-sensitive ads not only appear on your search but in your mail. Your mail is more you than your search. More and more of us are switching to Gmail because it brings context and hence meaning to our mail as well. Instead of an endless and meaningless list of entries, mail is being rearranged into contextual conversations.

Conversation will move into the center of the marketplace. Conversation will also redefine our understanding of information, of education, of health, and of community.

In the pre-blogging world of four years ago, all you would find in your search was a static document. Now, increasingly, you find a conversation.

We are just starting to understand that the explicit information located in a document is only a small part of the value. It is in the tacit information that emerges from conversation that the gold is found. It is in conversation, in the context of a legitimate relationship, that learning and the best value occurs.

Knowledge is not an object.

The idea that knowledge is an object is an industrial artifact. Knowledge is more than facts; it is about understanding and participation. Google enables you to find the best person and the best conversation. This is what is behind the marketing revolution. This is what is behind the impending revolution in education and health. Conversation is also the force behind the generation of a new community.

Google provides the connective tissue that will make important conversations and communities the paramount places of informed power in the world and will put dogma back into the waste bin of history.

Conversation, Voice, Community, And Identity

At the center of conversation is the blog.

At the heart of the blog is the authentic voice. The product of the authentic voice is community. The end game of community is identity. Identity is the answer of the greatest question that any human can ask: "Who am I?"

The machine world has progressively killed off our authentic voice. We instead struggle to fit into a machine structure that tells us who we should be rather than allowing us to become the person of destiny that we can be. We work to get marks at school rather than to learn about our world and our place in it. We end up in jobs where we give up ourselves. We are bombarded with messages that tell us what we should look like, what we should wear, who we should mate with, how to be happy, and who we should be. No wonder we find relationships difficult. How can we have a relationship with another when we have lost the core relationship with our own selves?

What is a blog then?

It is also a generative space in which we can give birth to our lost voice. As we find our voice, we begin to wake up. We start to become human again.

How does the blog awaken us? This open space invites us to speak in public. Hesitant, at first we speak the old way. But now and then the occasional real voice pops out. As it does, others notice and drop by and encourage us. Encouraged, we use our real voice more often. More people drop by and encourage us. Thank you, Peter and Critt—my first Angels.

Our voice is so strong that it can be heard around the entire globe. We are amazed to find others far away who can hear us and who have the same tone. Thank you, dear Dina.

Community begins to form. This is not about the communities of A-list bloggers with thousands of readers. This is about having a small group of fifteen or thirty strong connections with an inner circle of five to eight. As much as we expand our RSS reader lists, we find that we can only manage these limited numbers. Why? These are magic numbers. They are the core numbers of our ancient tribal hunter-gatherer past. It should be no surprise that we become most human again in the context that we are designed to be most comfortable in, the tribe.

Once again we begin to experience the ecstasy of communion with our spiritual brothers and sisters. I use the word communion because community is now too pallid a feeling. I use the word ecstasy because that is the power of the feeling. No wonder blogging is addictive. What could be more addictive than finding out who you are in communion with people that you trust completely? Your new identity as a human being emerges in the context of this community.

Power And The Web Of Life

Is this just a self-referencing talking shop? No. I am seeing powerful forces under way that demand action.

For tribes are not simply social organizations, like bridge clubs. Neither are they about work alone. Tribes are not separate from place, either. Most important, tribes know that wisdom comes from the group and that the future comes from their children. In the tribal world the wholeness is restored. The separations of the machine world are healed.

It is the tribes that will start to rebuild our culture and that will replace the machine institutions with new ones that support life. It is the network effect that will give these tribes power beyond their small cell size.

Imagine, the Web made flesh.

Like the Web itself, these interconnected tribes will have a resiliency and a power unimaginable to us today. If you doubt me, imagine the trajectory of the Open Source movement. Imagine what Wikipedia will be like in twenty years.

The power of this new Web will be enhanced by the release of the power of the full potential of each of us as humans. In the machine world we lived a drab life. But as free men and women who have found their true path and their community, what will our power be like?

Our Great Return

We are going home again to the place where humans fit.

Just as people at the end of the Middle Ages rediscovered the wisdom of the Classic world, so we are rediscovering the experience of tribal life. I don't mean by this that we will have to take up hunting and live in caves. For we have made a Great Return before and we know how it will play out. Renaissance men did not put on togas. What they did was to remember the wisdom of the Classic world that had been forgotten in a millennium-long dark age and applied this wisdom to the world of their time. So we too will begin to experience a new way of living and of being and apply this experience to our own time and to our own challenges.

There will come a time when humanity will choose to go against nature, to exploit her bounteous gifts, causing a sickness across the planet. People will forget the ecstasies of communion, and life will become drab and colorless.

In these coming dark ages, though, a deep sense of loss will cause the beginnings of a Great Return. They will look at the landscape and the old temples, built to withstand the cataclysms of millennia and understand once again the sacred laws of Existence.

When this day comes, humanity will have come of age. It will consciously acknowledge its role in the creative impulse that comes from the Sun, fertilizes the Earth, and calls forth the flame in the hearts of men and women to worship Life and the miraculous forces behind Creation.

—Hamish Miller and Paul Broadhurst, *The Sun and the Serpent*

From The Editor

We originally had one open spot in the project. We actually accepted two *More Space* proposals. Robert was added because his proposal was so compelling. It is so hard to say what is more interesting about Robert, where he has been or where he is going. He's been a diamond prospector in Botswana as well as an investment banker in London. Today, he is working to build communities on Prince Edward Island. The Queen Street Commons, where he lives, is a model for building communities of free agents.

In His Own Words . . .

What is it about your essay topic that made you want to write this chapter in *More Space*?

"I wanted to make sense of what I feel is going on around us. I wanted in particular to set an agenda for my own actions and for my own work. I want to be part of a group that will use this insight to help my own community rise from the ashes of a failed industrial experiment and find again the power and self-respect embedded in its roots and history. My hope is that by describing a possible future, I can help it emerge. And my thrill is that even now, only months after a first draft, parts of what I wrote about are indeed beginning to happen."

Robert's blog:
smartpei.typepad.com

Robert's favorite blogs:
www.experiencedesignernetwork.com

www.fragmentsfromfloyd.com

www.roundourhouse.com/blog

Recommended reading:
The Hidden Connections—Integrating the Biological, Cognitive and Social Dimensions of Life into a Science of Sustainability
by Fritjof Capra

The Nature of Order: "An Essay on the Art Of Building and the Nature of the Universe" (in four volumes)
by Christopher Alexander

How Children Fail
by John Holt

CREDITS

Edited by
Todd Sattersten

Written by
Jory Des Jardins, Lisa Haneberg, Rob May, Johnnie Moore, Marc Orchant, Robert Paterson, Evelyn Rodriguez, Curt Rosengren, Jeremy Wright

Designed by
Tim Frame

Photography by
Mark Ahn, Peter Chen, Paige Falk, Richard J. Gerstner, Joe Gough, Jason Hone, Gareth Lawrence, Jeffrey McDonald, Cristian Nitu, Amanda Rohde, Paulus Rusyanto, Leah-Anne Thompson

Printed by
INLAND BOOK

Everything else by
Amy Buckley

Special thanks to
Tom Ehrenfeld, Jack Covert, Hilary Powers, Sharon Rice and Seth Godin

This text was produced under the following criteria:

Trim Size: 8"x10" Portrait.
Binding: Perfect.
Cover: 10 pt. C1S Kalima Paper, 4 Color, Lay Flat Polyester Gloss Film Lamination.
Paper: 70 lb. Lynx Opaque, Uncoated/Off-set.
Font Colors: Black and Orange (PMS 144U).
Font Types: Garamond10/12 and Trade Gothic Bold Condensed10.5/15.
Photographs: 4 Color.

Astronaut
PROJECTS